Lots & Lots of FIRE TRUCKS & FIREFIGHTERS™

by Tom DeMichael & Tom Edinger

Marshall Publishing & Promotions, Inc.

Barrington, Illinois

Written by Tom DeMichael and Tom Edinger
Edited by Tom DeMichael
Book and Graphic Design by Tom DeMichael and Tom Edinger

Text and design copyright © 2008 Marshall Publishing and Promotions, Inc.

MARSHALL PUBLISHING AND PROMOTIONS, INC.
123 S. HOUGH ST.
BARRINGTON, IL 60010
www.marshallpublishinginc.com

ISBN 978-0-9789286-7-4
Library of Congress Control Number: 2007922957
Printed in China

Our thanks to Pierce Manufacturing, Appleton, WI; Clarendon Hills Fire Department, Clarendon Hills, IL; Aurora Regional Fire Museum, Aurora, IL; John Hanley & Toronto Fire Pix; Houston Fire Museum, Houston, TX, Mike Madden, K. Corey Keeble, Royal Ontario Museum; Alexa, Eliza, Nemea, Nikko, and Steve.

Photo credits
Cover: Pierce Manufacturing, Jack Edinger
Back Cover: Pierce Manufacturing, Jack Edinger, John Hanley
3 – 6 Jack Edinger
11 – 26 Pierce Manufacturing, Jack Edinger, John Hanley
27 – 32 Pierce Manufacturing, Tom Edinger, John Hanley, National Fire Prevention Association (NFPA,) Prints and Photographs Division – Library of Congress, Public Domain
33 – 36 Public Domain
37 – 38 Public Domain, NFPA
39 – 44 Jack Edinger, Tom Edinger, NFPA
45 – 46 Aurora Regional Fire Museum, Pierce Manufacturing
47 – 52 Aurora Regional Fire Museum, John Hanley, Houston Fire Museum, Jack Edinger
53 – 58 John Hanley
59 – 62 Aurora Regional Fire Museum, Public Domain
63 – 68 Aurora Regional Fire Museum, Public Domain, Tom Edinger
69 – 72 Aurora Regional Fire Museum, Public Domain, Pierce Manufacturing
73 – 76 John Naughton
77 – 82 Public Domain, Tom Edinger, U.S. Navy Photo by Photographer's Mate 2nd Class Jim Watson
83 – 104 Public Domain, Prints and Photographs Division – Library of Congress
105 – 114 Manchester Fire Museum, Aurora Regional Fire Museum, Hose 5 Fire Museum, Boston Fire Museum, Greenville Old Firehouse Museum, Comstock Firemen's Museum, Brookhaven Fire Museum, Firefighters' Memorial Museum, Fire Museum of York County, Texas Fire Museum, Utah Museum of Fire Service History & Firefighter Memorial, Old Firehouse & Police Museum
115 – 122 Jack Edinger, John Hanley, Pierce Manufacturing
123 – Tom Edinger

This is for Paula, Anthony, and Alex - may they always stay safe, and my good friends, Tom and Mark. And to people like Vito and Ralph, who have my admiration and gratitude for putting themselves in harm's way everyday for their neighbors. - Tom DeMichael

For Katie, Jack, Joe and his family, Eleanora, Tom, Mark, and Jeff for without their support, love and friendship this book could not have been produced. Thank you and love to all. – Tom Edinger

We wish to honor all those who serve in the emergency response industry and thank you for standing tall and proud and risking your lives everyday so that we may all rest easy in our daily lives.

Table of Contents

Chapter 1
Meet Firefighter Joe

Hi everyone – meet Firefighter Joe – your host for your trip through the world of "Lots and Lots of Fire Trucks and Firefighters." Fireman Joe is one of over 1 million full-time and volunteer firefighters in service in the United States today. In real life, Joe is a good father and husband, works as a salesman and spends much of his free time at the firehouse, volunteering for firefighting service. Joe is usually at the firehouse for a 24 hour period during which he will eat, sleep, and stay trained on all the latest news and techniques for fighting fires and emergency rescues.

When he's not on call waiting for the emergency bell to ring, Joe has other duties at the fire house. He may work on the fire trucks and equipment, making sure they are kept spotlessly clean and in perfect working order. He may give a tour of the fire house to a class from school or a group of people from the community like a church, Boy or Girl Scouts, senior clubs and others. He may also be assigned by the chief to cook one of the meals or clean-up around the living quarters.

Fire fighters today do much more than just put out fires and get cats out of trees. When you call 911 for help, fire fighters may be called to the scene.

If there's a car accident, if someone has a heart attack, if there is a gas leak, or if someone is trapped in a high rise apartment, fire fighters are trained to help rescue those in need of help.

Everyone wants to know about the "fire pole." Did you know that fire fighters in the old days used the fire pole because they slept above the horses (the smell from the horses was pretty bad) and they needed to get downstairs as quickly as possible? It's true. In 1878, fire trucks were pulled by horses. At first the pole was considered a great time-saver but many fire fighters ended up with broken or sprained ankles and shins, so they soon put foam padding at the bottom of the pole. Most fire houses today have stairs and the fire fighters make it to the trucks just as fast as those going down the poles.

Day or night, once the fire bell rings, the fire fighters rush to put on their gear. A firefighter's gear (personal protective equipment - PPE) can weigh up to 80 pounds and they have to put all the protective clothing on within 30 seconds – that's almost as long as it takes most people to just get out of bed!!

Let's take a look at how Fireman Joe gets ready for an emergency call.

Cotton t-shirt protects Firefighter Joe from the heat of the fire and also keeps him cool during the hot summer months. His pants and shoes are made of special materials that resist heat and fire.

His black rubber turnout boots are heavy, with steel toes and a steel foot plate for protection. They make sure his feet are clean, dry, and safe.

These are turnout pants. They're called "turnouts" because Firefighter Joe keeps them turned inside-out with his boots attached. In an emergency, he can jump right into his boots and pull up the pants. His turnouts are held up by traditional red suspenders and have pockets for tools and gloves. The pants are made of Nomex® and other fire protective materials.

The tank that Firefighter Joe wears on his back is called a SCBA tank – Self Contained Breathing Apparatus (much like skin divers use underwater.) A burning building can be full of hot gases and smoke – the SCBA tank lets Joe breathe fresh air for about 30 minutes while he's fighting the fire.

The SCBA mask is a very important part of the breathing unit. It delivers the oxygen to Joe's mouth and nose. The special plastic face shield protects Joe from hot gases and smoke, as well as fire and crackling ashes.

Firefighter Joe's helmet protects his head from falling debris and helps other firefighters identify him through the smoke and flames. Chiefs and senior officers wear a white helmet; captains' helmets are red; firefighters' helmets are black or yellow. Everyone has their own bright white number on the helmet. The helmet also has a light on it to help the firefighters see at night and in dark buildings.

The turnout coat is made of several layers, inside and out, that protects Firefighter Joe from fire. It also keeps him warm and dry from icy water when he's fighting a fire in the freezing cold. Like his pants, the coat is made of Nomex®. The bright reflecting stripes help other firefighters see Joe at night or in a dark building. The coat also has a Nomex® hood that covers Joe's head.

The gloves are usually the last item that Firefighter Joe puts on. Like everything else he wears, they are made of fire protective materials and keep Joe safe from fire and sharp objects.

Lots & Lots of FIRE TRUCKS & FIREFIGHTERS

Chapter 2
Firefighter's Tools & Equipment

Firefighters like Joe have to use all kinds of different tools and machines to rescue people from burning buildings, car wrecks, and other kinds of accidents and emergencies. There are special tools that can help a firefighter pry open a door or cut through metal to rescue someone. Cutting tools like saws and axes help firefighters help people who are trapped in a house on fire.

The **HALLIGAN** (also known as a **HALLIGAN TOOL or BAR**) is a special pry bar that allows firefighters to open doors and windows that may be locked or stuck. It also can be used to twist off knobs, punch holes in glass or wood, or pull a lock cylinder. Its name comes from the New York City Fire Chief who invented it in 1948 – Hugh Halligan. It may be the most used firefighting tool in the world.

The **BATTERING RAM** is a large, heavy steel pole that can be used by one or two firefighters to quickly break down a door. The weight of the ram is between 35 and 45 pounds and, along with the momentum of the ram, it makes easy work of entering burning buildings.

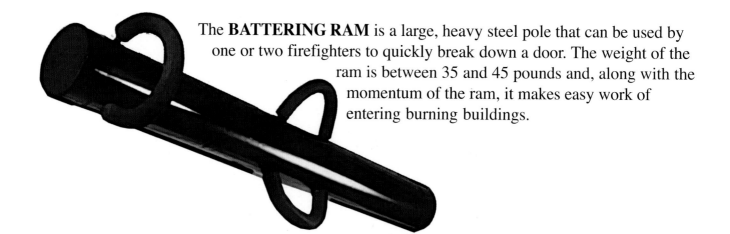

The **AXE** comes in two varieties for firefighters.

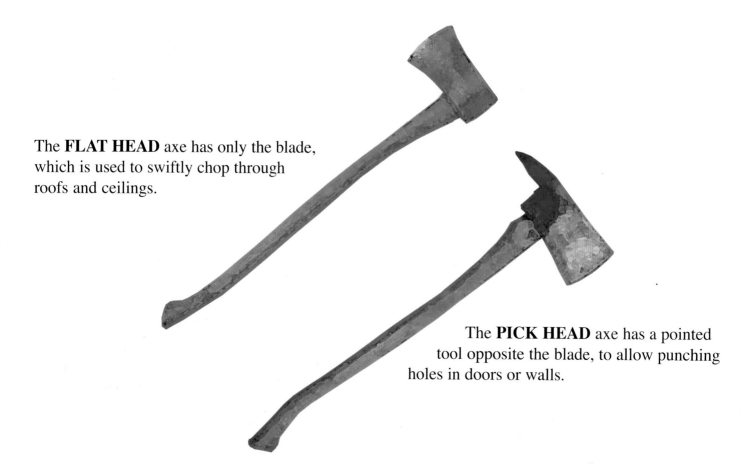

The **FLAT HEAD** axe has only the blade, which is used to swiftly chop through roofs and ceilings.

The **PICK HEAD** axe has a pointed tool opposite the blade, to allow punching holes in doors or walls.

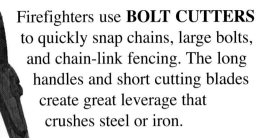

Firefighters use **BOLT CUTTERS** to quickly snap chains, large bolts, and chain-link fencing. The long handles and short cutting blades create great leverage that crushes steel or iron.

PIKE POLES are anywhere from six to twelve feet long and are used to pull down sections of wallboard or sheetrock in burning buildings. Firefighters must get behind these walls, as fires can smolder and wooden studs can burn without ever being seen.

Hydraulic rescue tools, the most famous of which is known as the brand name **"JAWS OF LIFE,"** have become a very valuable part of the emergency team. The use of a hydraulic piston forces steel jaws to open and close with enormous force. Combination tools can quickly cut through the steel posts of a car, then spread a mangled door open with the same amazing strength. They were originally designed in 1972 by Hurst Performance Inc. for race car emergencies. It is estimated that more than 35,000 Jaws of Life systems are in operation around the world.

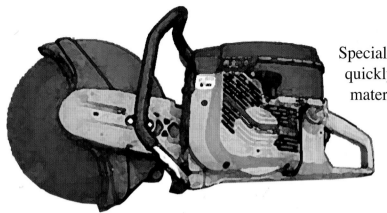

Special **CIRCULAR SAWS** and chain saws can quickly cut through wood, steel, and other tough materials to release those who are trapped.

Large portable **FANS** (sometimes refered to as **SMOKE EJECTORS**) can be used to exhaust smoke and toxic gases quickly from an enclosed area.

PORTABLE GENERATORS are helpful where regular electric service is not available or usable. Many life-saving tools rely on the energy produced by these generators.

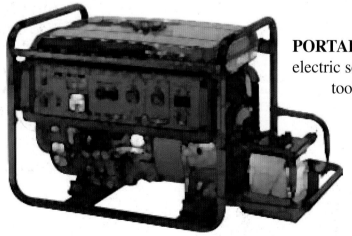

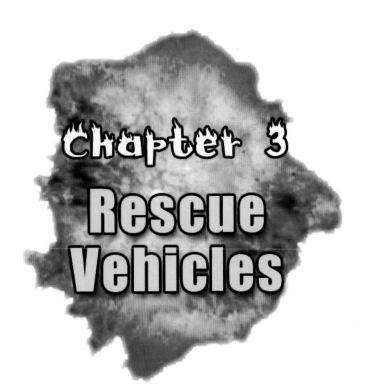

Chapter 3
Rescue Vehicles

Pumper Trucks

Let's start with a closer look at the fire truck that pumps the water from the fire hydrant to the fire ...it's called the *pumper truck* and it's the one you see most of the time. They're often called an *engine*, dating back to the time when steam engines powered the pump that pressurized water - even though the vehicle was horse-drawn.

Pumper trucks are about 30 feet long, can carry up to 1,000 gallons of water and they also carry hundreds of feet of fire hose. Pumper trucks are usually the first trucks to arrive at the scene of a fire or emergency.

Firefighters always work together as a team to put out the fire as fast as they can to make sure that no one gets hurt. When a pumper truck arrives at a fire the driver parks the truck as close to a fire hydrant as possible or other water source such as a lake or pond in areas

outside a city. That's why it's important to never block the area in front of a fire hydrant. The firefighter will then attach a big six-inch diameter hose to send the water into the pumper tank. Water that's been stored in the engine's tank or drawn in through an outside source is then sent through a pump on the truck and forced out at high pressure to the hoses which are connected at various points around the truck. It can take up to four firefighters to handle a large fire hose.

Lots & Lots of FIRE TRUCKS & FIREFIGHTERS

Some pumper trucks might look a little different but they all do the same important job – they get the water to the fire to put it out. Some trucks also have a foam system that carries about 20 gallons of foam. There are two different kinds of foam – Class A which is used to smother the flames inside a

building to keep them from re-igniting and Class B foam which is used to fight car fires or other flammable liquid fires.

It's important to always get out of the way when you hear loud sirens or see the flashing lights of a rescue vehicle, whether you're on foot or riding in a car. While the engines appear to be going very fast, they rarely travel much faster than normal traffic - but they do take longer and need more distance to stop. You should always give emergency vehicles extra room.

With different fire departments having varying needs, fire engines come in all shapes, sizes and colors! On the following pages you'll see all kinds of Pumper Trucks!

Lots & Lots of FIRE TRUCKS & FIREFIGHTERS

Lots & Lots of **FIRE TRUCKS & FIREFIGHTERS**

Lots & Lots of FIRE TRUCKS & FIREFIGHTERS

Rescue Vehicles

Ladder Trucks

Probably the most spectacular fire truck you'll see in action is the aerial *ladder truck*. There's no better way for a firefighter to get from down on the ground to way up in the sky. It's what firefighters call the "big stick."

A ladder truck is quite a large vehicle, usually about 40 to 50 feet long. The ladder on the truck is about 100 feet long and can go as high as 10 floors, stretching up the outside of an apartment or factory building. The end of some ladders have a bucket or platform where the firefighters can stand and aim the water onto the fire.

The ladder truck is used to rescue people from a fire or to get firefighters to difficult to reach places. In addition, they can pour large amounts of water from the stick to help putting out the fire.

Four jacks or stabilizers on the sides of the aerial ladder truck help to make sure the weight of the ladder doesn't cause the truck to tip over. On some ladder trucks, like those built by

Pierce Manufacturing and others, the ladder has a 3-inch pipe that runs to the top of the ladder. This pipe can spray up to 1000 gallons of water per minute to wherever the firefighter points the stream.

Tiller ladder trucks have ladders that can expand like a telescope, reaching up in the air to about 100 feet. The tiller truck also has two steering wheels and two drivers - one in the

front and one in the back. The one in the back controls the rear wheels of the truck, and allows this very long truck to go around corners easily.

Just like the pumper truck, there are all kinds of aerial ladder trucks – let's take a look at them...

Lots & Lots of **FIRE TRUCKS & FIREFIGHTERS**

Lots & Lots of **FIRE TRUCKS & FIREFIGHTERS**

Lots & Lots of **FIRE TRUCKS & FIREFIGHTERS**

Rescue Vehicles

Specialty Vehicles

Lots & Lots of **FIRE TRUCKS & FIREFIGHTERS**

Did you know that firefighters don't just fight fires? They often rescue people from accidents - especially if someone is trapped. Some fire trucks carry medical supplies and rescue equipment. We call this type of fire truck a *specialty truck*.

There are many different kinds of specialty vehicles. A *First Response Rescue Unit* is used to manage emergency scenes until more equipment and personnel can arrive. *Urban Search and Rescue Units* are specially designed to handle natural and man-made disasters. A *Hazmat Response Unit* handles the threat of hazardous material spills. *Air and Light Support* vehicles provide breathing

and lighting assistance to firefighters and rescue crews. *Bomb Response* vehicles handle the dangerous task of controlling and collecting explosives. *Heavy-Duty Rescue* vehicles are mobile storage units, capable of carrying equipment like tools, ladders, breathing tanks, medical supplies and more.

There are fire trucks and there are fireboats. Fireboats are used to fight fires on the water or near the shore. On many fireboats, firefighters can make their way up into a tall tower mounted to the boat. From up there, firefighters can spray thousands of gallons of water per minute onto a blazing fire, drawing directly from the bay or harbor.

Lots & Lots of FIRE TRUCKS & FIREFIGHTERS

Other specialty rescue vehicles include helicopters and airplanes that have buckets or tanks. These aerial vehicles can deliver thousands of gallons of water scooped from lakes or fire retardant chemicals to control fires from the air. Firefighters also use all-terrain vehicles, jeeps, and even motorcycles that can make their way into almost any kind of land environment.

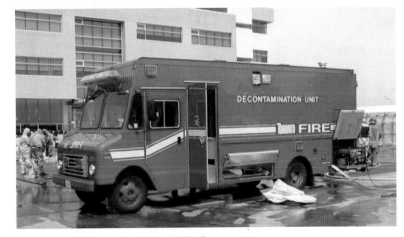

Lots & Lots of FIRE TRUCKS & FIREFIGHTERS

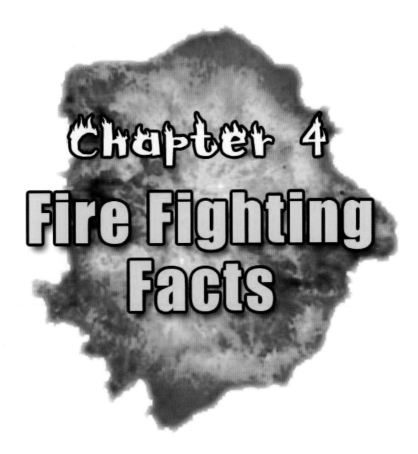

Chapter 4
Fire Fighting Facts

In the United States in 2006…

- A fire department responded to a fire every 19 seconds.

- One structure fire was reported every 62 seconds.

- One home structure fire was reported every 83 seconds.

- One civilian fire injury was reported every 29 minutes.

- One civilian fire death occurred every 2 hours and 23 minutes.

- One outside fire was reported every 39 seconds.

- One vehicle fire was reported every 109 seconds.

(Please note: As the volume and expanse of American fire and firefighting statistics are so enormous and take time to compile, 2006 data are the most recent available at press time.)

The U.S. fire service (2006)

- 1,140,900 firefighters protected the United States in 2006. 316,950 (28%) are career firefighters and 823,950 (72%) are volunteer firefighters.

- Most career firefighters (74%) are in communities that protect 25,000 or more people.

- Most volunteer firefighters (95%) are in departments that protect fewer than 25,000 people and more than half are located in small, rural departments that protect fewer than 2,500 people.

- There are an estimated 30,635 fire departments in the United States. These fire departments have an estimated 53,200 fire stations, 69,300 pumpers, and 6,700 aerial apparatus.

- Medical aid calls have nearly tripled since 1980.

Firefighter fatalities (2006)

- There were 89 firefighter deaths in 2006.

- Stress and overexertion, which usually results in heart attacks or other sudden cardiac events, continue to be the leading cause of fatal injury. Of the 38 stress-related deaths in 2006, 34 were classified as sudden cardiac deaths.

- Wildland fires accounted for the largest share of fireground deaths with 16.

- Fireground operations accounted for 38 deaths.

- Nineteen firefighters died in vehicle crashes, while three others were fatally struck by vehicles and one firefighter fell from a vehicle.

Firefighter injuries (2006)

- There were 83,400 firefighter injuries in 2006.

- 44,210 (53%) of all firefighter injuries occurred during fireground operations. An estimated 13,690 occurred during other on duty activities, while 13,090 occurred at non-fire emergency incidents.

- The major types of injuries received during fireground operations were: strain, sprain, wound, cut, bleeding, bruise, burns, smoke or gas inhalation and thermal stress.

- Falls, slipping, or jumping (23.9%) and overexertion or strain (25.5%) were the leading causes of fireground injuries in firefighters.

- Regionally, the Northeast had the highest fireground injury rate with 5.0 injuries occurring per 100 fires; this was more than twice the rate for the rest of country.

Arson

Arson, as it is known today, is best measured by intentionally-set fires. The number of U.S. reported intentional structure fires fell to 37,500 in 2003, down from 160,000 incendiary or suspicious structure fires reported in 1978 and down 68% from the more-comparable 115,700 incendiary structure fires in 1978. These figures do not include adjustments for fires with cause undetermined or unreported (see first bullet below for adjusted statistics). Arson has consistently had the highest rate of juvenile involvement compared with all other FBI-indexed crimes (the most serious felonies).

Facts & figures

- There were an estimated 68,800 intentional structure fires in 2002. These fires resulted in 630 civilian deaths, 2,030 civilian injuries, and $1.9 billion in direct property damage.

- There were an estimated 62,300 intentional vehicle fires in 2002. These fires resulted in 100 civilian deaths, 120 civilian injuries and $380 million in direct property damage.

- For the ninth straight year, juvenile fire-setters accounted for roughly half (at least 49%) or more of those arrested for arson. In 2003, 51% of those apprehended were under 18, nearly one-third were under the age of 15, and 3% were under the age of 10, according to the FBI.

- According to FBI statistics, only 17% of 2003 arson offenses were cleared (solved) by arrest. Juvenile offenders accounted for the only arrestees for 41% of these clearances. An estimated 2% of intentional fires led to convictions.

- Intentional fires ranked first among the major causes in structure fire dollar loss between 1999 and 2002.

Cooking safety

Cooking fires are the #1 cause of home fires and home fire injuries. Most cooking equipment fires start with the ignition of common household items (i.e., food or grease, cabinets, wall coverings, paper or plastic bags, curtains, etc.)

Facts & figures

- In 2005, U.S. fire departments responded to 146,400 home structure fires that involved cooking equipment in 2005. These fires caused 480 civilian fire deaths, 4,690 civilian fire injuries and $876 million in direct property damage.

- Unattended cooking is the leading cause of home cooking fires.

- Three in 10 reported home fires start in the kitchen — more than any other place in the home.

- Two out of three reported home cooking fires start with the range or stove.

- Electric ranges or stoves have a higher risk of fires, injuries and property damage, compared to gas ranges or stoves, but gas ranges or stoves have a higher risk of fire deaths.

Christmas tree fires

Christmas trees that are carefully decorated can help make your holidays safer. **Note:** These statistics are based on fires that started with Christmas trees and do not include fires starting with other products. A small fire that spreads to a Christmas tree can very quickly become large.

Facts & figures

- Christmas trees were the items first ignited in an estimated average of 210 reported U.S. home structure fires per year in 2002-2005. These fires caused an average of 24 civilian deaths, 27 civilian injuries, and $13.3 million in direct property damage per year. These statistics include both real and artificial trees.

- On average, one in every 9 reported home Christmas tree fires resulted in a death.

- Almost half (48%) of home Christmas tree fires are caused by electrical problems or malfunctions. Twenty-seven percent of home Christmas tree fires resulted from a heat source placed too close to the tree. Five percent were started by children playing with fire.

- Holiday lights (or other decorative lighting with live voltage) were involved in 22% of the home Christmas tree structure fires. Fixed or portable space heaters were involved in 7% of these incidents. No equipment was involved in 36% of these fires.

- Candles were the heat source in 15% of the home Christmas tree fires per year between 2002 and 2005.

- Two-thirds of the home Christmas tree fires were reported in the month of December, 19% were reported in January.

- During the same five-year period, 90 outside or unclassified fires began with Christmas trees, on average, per year. Sixty-four percent of the outside and unclassified home Christmas tree fires were intentionally set. Two-thirds of these firesoccurred in January.

Forest and Wildland fires (2005)

In terms of America's national resources, the 2005 forest and wildfire fire season was moderate.

Facts & Figures
- A total of 66,753 fires were reported resulting in a record of 8,689,389 acres burned.
- The highest number of fires for 2005 were located in the southern states.
- The highest number of acres burned were in the Western Great Basin.
- Alaska reported about 51 percent of the total number of acres burned.
- A National Fire Plan was developed in August 2000, following a landmark wildland fire season, with the intent of actively responding to severe wildland fires and their impacts to communities, while ensuring sufficient firefighting capacity for the future.

Lots & Lots of **FIRE TRUCKS & FIREFIGHTERS**

Chapter 5
Fire Science Basics

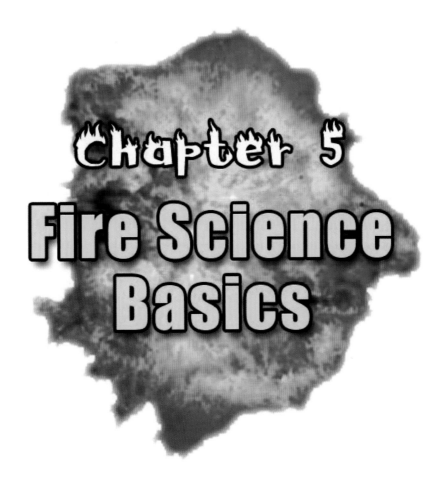

The ancient Greeks considered fire one of the major elements in the universe, alongside water, earth and air. But, unlike the other three, fire is not matter – it is matter changing its form – it's a chemical reaction.

Typically, fire comes from a chemical reaction between **oxygen** in the atmosphere and some sort of **fuel** (wood or gasoline, for example). Of course, wood and gasoline don't spontaneously catch on fire just because they're surrounded by oxygen. For the combustion reaction to happen, you have to **heat** the fuel to its ignition temperature. These three elements – fuel, oxygen, and heat – form what is known as the "Fire Triangle."

FIRE TRIANGLE

OXYGEN

HEAT

COMBUSTION

FUEL

smoke

heat

fire

char

ash

Here's the sequence of events in a typical wood fire:

Something heats the wood to a very high temperature. The heat can come from lots of different things — a match, focused light, friction, lightning, or something else that is already burning.

When the wood reaches about 300 degrees Fahrenheit (150 degrees Celsius), the heat decomposes some of the cellulose material that makes up the wood.

Some of the decomposed material is released as volatile gases. We know these gases as smoke. **Smoke** is a compound of hydrogen, carbon and oxygen. The rest of the material forms **char**, which is nearly pure carbon, and **ash**, which is all of the unburnable minerals in the wood (calcium, potassium, and so on). The char is what you buy when you buy charcoal. Charcoal is wood that has been heated to remove nearly all of the volatile gases and leave behind the carbon. That is why a charcoal fire burns with no smoke.

The actual burning of wood then happens in two separate reactions:

- When the volatile gases are hot enough (about 500 degrees F (260 degrees C) for wood), the compound molecules break apart, and the atoms recombine with the oxygen to form water, carbon dioxide and other products. In other words, they burn as **fire**.

- The carbon in the char combines with oxygen as well, and this is a much slower reaction. That is why charcoal in a BBQ can stay hot for a long time.

A side effect of these chemical reactions is a lot of **heat**. The fact that the chemical reactions in a fire generate a lot of <u>new</u> heat is what sustains the fire.

So, what kind of fuel will burn? Many common materials can act as fuels and they come in many different forms. Some are gases, like methane and propane, the fuels we burn in a stove, a furnace, or a camping stove. Some are liquids like gasoline and diesel, the fuels we burn in engines. And some are solids like wood and coal, the fuels we burn in fireplaces. But many other materials can be fuels. Many plastics are fuels. Paper and cotton are fuels. There are fuels all around the home and the workplace – in furniture, in bedding, in curtains, and on desks.

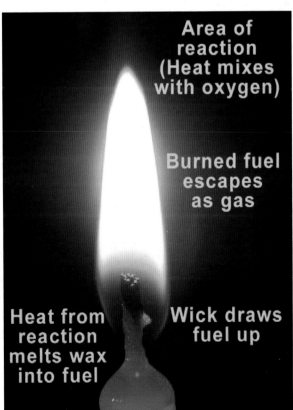

Area of reaction (Heat mixes with oxygen)

Burned fuel escapes as gas

Heat from reaction melts wax into fuel

Wick draws fuel up

Gases that are fuels burn easily because the gas and the oxygen can mix easily and the heat generated encourages further burning.

For a liquid to burn, the heat from the fire must boil off some of the fuel so that it becomes a vapor and can mix with the oxygen in the air.

For a solid fuel to burn, the heat from the fire has to decompose fuel into vapors that can mix with oxygen in the air.

Chapter 6
Fire Prevention Week

It all started on October 9, 1911, when Fire Prevention Day was inaugurated in America. The date of October 9 was chosen because it marked the anniversary of the "Great Chicago Fire of 1871" — the disaster that killed 250 people and destroyed 17,430 buildings at a cost of $168 million. It was the fire that started people thinking in terms of fire *prevention* rather than just firefighting.

Fire Prevention Day was begun by the Fire Marshals Association of North America (now part of the National Fire Protection Association (NFPA.) The day was first proclaimed by

President Woodrow Wilson on the 40th anniversary of the Chicago blaze. In 1922, on recommendation of a member of NFPA and unanimous vote of the membership at the association's annual meeting that year, the fire safety observance was extended to cover the entire week that includes the October 9

anniversary date. President Warren Harding was the first to officially proclaim National Fire Prevention Week.

NFPA continues to be the international sponsor of Fire Prevention Week, which is always the Sunday-through-Saturday period during which the October 9 anniversary date falls. According to the National Archives and Records Administration's Library Information Center, Fire Prevention Week is the longest running public health and safety observance on record.

Chapter 7
Fire Prevention & Safety Tips

FIRE PREVENTION AND SAFETY TIPS FROM FIREFIGHTER JOE...
Firefighter Joe believes the best way to stay out of a fire is to practice good fire prevention and safety tips. Whether it's around your house, school, business, church, or other structure, following good fire prevention practices is the best way to keep you safe, all year round.

FIRE PREVENTION AT HOME:
More than 4,000 Americans die each year in fires and approximately 20,000 are injured. An overwhelming number of fires occur in the home. There are time-tested ways to prevent a fire at home. It's merely a matter of planning ahead.

Every Home Should Have at Least One Working Smoke Alarm
Buy a smoke alarm at any hardware or discount store. It's inexpensive protection for you and your family. Install a smoke alarm on every level of your home. A working smoke alarm can double your chances of survival. Test it monthly, keep it free of dust and replace the battery at least twice a year (usually when clocks are

adjusted for daylight savings time.) Smoke alarms themselves should be replaced after ten years of service, or as recommended by the manufacturer.

Prevent Electrical Fires
Never overload circuits or extension cords. Do not place cords and wires under rugs, over nails or in high traffic areas. Immediately shut off and unplug appliances that sputter, spark or emit an unusual smell. Have them professionally repaired or replaced.

Use Appliances Wisely
When using appliances, follow the manufacturer's safety precautions. Overheating, unusual smells, shorts and sparks are all warning signs that appliances need to be shut off, then replaced or repaired. Unplug appliances when not in use. Use safety caps to cover all unused outlets, especially if there are small children in the home.

Alternate Heaters
Portable heaters need their space. Keep anything combustible at least three feet away. Keep fire in the fireplace. Use fire screens and have your chimney cleaned annually. The creosote buildup can ignite a chimney fire that could easily spread. Kerosene heaters should be used only where approved by authorities. Never use gasoline or camp-stove fuel. Refuel outside and only after the heater has cooled.

Smoking
Careless smoking is the leading cause of fire deaths and the second leading cause of injuries among people ages 65 and older. Cigarettes will continue to burn when they are not properly extinguished. When a resting cigarette is accidentally knocked over, it can smolder for hours before a flare-up occurs. Before you light your next cigarette, remember:
- Put your cigarette or cigar out at the first sign of feeling drowsy while watching television or reading.
- Use deep ashtrays and put your cigarette all the way out.
- Never smoke in bed.
- Don't walk away from lit cigarettes and other smoking materials.
- Don't put ashtrays on the arms of sofas or chairs.

FIRE SAFETY AT HOME:

Establish your own Operation **E.D.I.T.H.** Plan – **Exit Drills In The Home.** Here's how to make your own Operation EDITH Plan:

Appoint a Fire Chief. The Fire Chief can be your father, mother, teen-aged brother or sister, or even the babysitter.

The family visits each bedroom and picks 2 WAYS OUT- one the normal way out and the other emergency route, through a different door or window.

Plan how each member of the family can reach the ground floor using the emergency route.

Decide on a meeting place outside the house such as near the mailbox or driveway.

Draw a picture of each floor in your home. Show where the rooms, doors, windows, and halls are. Then color the regular escape routes black and the emergency routes red. Copies should be placed where everyone can see them and be reminded of what to do in a fire emergency. Be sure the upper floors have an escape ladder available.

Hold a family meeting and discuss the following topics:
Always sleep with the bedroom doors closed. This will keep deadly heat and smoke out of bedrooms, giving you additional time to escape.

Keep flashlihgts with fresh batteries by your bedside - in case of power failure or heavy smoke, it will help you find your way out.

Find a way for everyone to sound a family alarm. Yelling, pounding on walls, whistles, etc. Practice yelling "FIRE!"

In a fire, time is critical. Don't waste time getting dressed, don't search for pets or valuables. Just get out!

Roll out of bed. Stay low. One breath of smoke or gases may be enough to kill.

Be sure to plan ahead:
Practice evacuating the building blindfolded. In a real fire situation, the amount of smoke generated by a fire most likely will make it difficult to see.

Practice staying low to the ground when escaping.

Always check a closed door with the back of your hand BEFORE opening - if it's warm or hot to the touch, leave it CLOSED and try a different route.

Learn to STOP, DROP to the ground, and ROLL if clothes catch fire.

FIRE SAFETY TIPS DURING THE HOLIDAY SEASON:
Keep matches, lighters, and candles out of the reach of children.
If children are participating in Hanukkah, Kwanzaa, or Advent candle-lighting ceremonies in your home, make sure they are being supervised by an adult.

Practice your Operation E.D.I.T.H Plan during the holidays. Visiting friends and family members will need to know two ways out if there is a fire emergency in your home.

Use only decorative lights that have been tested for safety. Look for the UL Label from Underwriters Laboratories on the light cords.

Check each set of lights for broken or cracked sockets, frayed or bare wires, and/or loose connections. If there is any question about the safety of the light set, it should be thrown away.

Check the labels on the light set for inside or outside use. Never use inside lights outside. Be sure to fasten your outside light sets tightly so they will not be damaged by the wind. The wind can cause the wires to fray, break, and cause an electrical short circuit.

Read the manufacturers instructions carefully. Do not use more than the recommended number of lights on a circuit.

Always turn off your lights on trees or on paper decorations before going out or going to bed. If there is a short circuit, a fire may start.

Keep children away from decorative lights and electrical decorations.

Always throw wrapping paper away immediately after opening a package.

Never burn wrapping paper in the fireplace. The paper can catch fire very quickly and cause a flash fire.

Never use candles on a tree, near evergreens, near paper decorations, or near wrapping paper.

Always use non-flammable candle-holders, Kinara, Advent wreaths, and Menorahs.

Always place candles where they cannot be knocked down or blown over. Don't forget about them. If candles are in a centerpiece on your holiday table, don't let them melt down into the decorations. That may cause a fire.

IMPORTANT: Make sure your emergency phone numbers are placed next to or on the telephone. Make sure that everyone knows where they are.

Check your fire extinguisher regularly to be sure that it is full and working properly. Make sure that everyone knows where it is and how to use it.

FIRE EXTINGUISHERS:
There are three different basic types of fire extinguishers, based on the type of fire they can safely and properly put out.

Class A Extinguishers will put out fires in ordinary combustibles, such as wood and paper.

Class B Extinguishers should be used on fires involving flammable liquids, such as grease, gasoline, oil, etc.

Class C Extinguishers are suitable for use on electrically energized fires.

Use a portable fire extinguisher when the fire is confined to a small area, such as a wastebasket, and is not growing; everyone has exited the building; the fire department has been called or is being called; and the room is not filled with smoke.

To operate a fire extinguisher, remember the word PASS:
- **P**ull the pin. Hold the extinguisher with the nozzle pointing away from you, and release the locking mechanism.
- **A**im low. Point the extinguisher at the base of the fire.
- **S**queeze the lever slowly and evenly.
- **S**weep the nozzle from side-to-side. For the home, select a multi-purpose extinguisher (ABC - can be used on all types of home fires) that is large enough to put out a small fire,

but not so heavy as to be difficult to handle.

Dry Chemical extinguishers are usually rated for multiple purpose use. They contain an extinguishing agent and use a compressed, non-flammable gas as a propellant.

Halon extinguishers contain a gas that interrupts the chemical reaction that takes place when fuels burn. These types of extinguishers are often used to protect valuable electrical equipment since they leave no residue to clean up. Halon extinguishers have a limited range, usually 4 to 6 feet. The initial application of Halon should be made at the base of the fire, even after the flames have been extinguished.

Water These extinguishers contain water and compressed gas and should only be used on Class A (ordinary combustibles) fires.

Carbon Dioxide (CO2) extinguishers are most effective on Class B and C (liquids and electrical) fires. Since the gas disperses quickly, these extinguishers are only effective from 3 to 8 feet. The carbon dioxide is stored as a compressed liquid in the extinguisher; as it expands, it cools the surrounding air. The cooling will often cause ice to form around the "horn" where the gas is expelled from the extinguisher. Since the fire could re-ignite, continue to apply the agent even after the fire appears to be out.

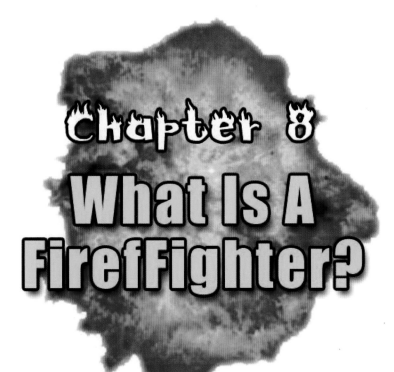

Chapter 8
What Is A FireFighter?

Very little is known about this legendary poem - the author is unknown. But it was written in the past, when traditional roles kept women in the household and men in the fire houses.

Today, this poem tells of the brave men AND women who make up the proud profession of firefighting.

He's the guy next door, a man's man with the memory of a little boy.

He's never gotten over the excitement of the engines and sirens and danger.

He's the guy like you and me with warts and worries and unfilled dreams. Yet he stands taller than most of us.

He's a fireman.

He puts it on the line when the bell rings. A fireman - at once the most fortunate and the least fortunate of men.

He's a man who saves lives, because he's seen too much death.

He's a gentle man because he has seen the awesome power of violence out of control.

He's responsive to a child's laughter, because his arms held too many small bodies that will never laugh again.

He's a simple man who enjoys the simple pleasures in life - hot coffee held in numb, unbending fingers, a warm bed for bone and muscle, compelled beyond feeling. The camraderie, of brave men and the divine peace and selfless service, of a job well done.

He doesn't wear buttons or wave flags or shout obscenities. When he marches, it's to honor a fallen comrade.

He doesn't preach the brotherhood of man - He lives it. - *Author Unknown*

Lots & Lots of FIRE TRUCKS & FIREFIGHTERS

Chapter 9
Firefighters in Action

Let's take a look at the brave men and women of yesterday and today, who risk their lives everyday - putting everything on the line to keep us safe...

Lots & Lots of **FIRE TRUCKS & FIREFIGHTERS**

Lots & Lots of **FIRE TRUCKS & FIREFIGHTERS**

Lots & Lots of **FIRE TRUCKS & FIREFIGHTERS**

Chapter 10
Words of the Firefighter

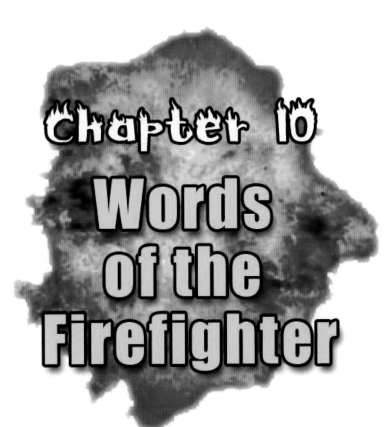

FIREMAN'S PRAYER

When I am called to duty, God, wherever flames may rage,

Give me strength to save some life, whatever be its age.

Help me embrace a little child before it is too late, or save an older person from the horror of that fate.

Enable me to be alert and hear the weakest shout, and quickly and efficiently to put the fire out.

I want to fill my calling and to give the best in me, to guard my every neighbor and protect his property.

And if according to my fate, I am to lose my life, please bless with your protecting hand, my children and my wife.

Author - Unknown

FIREMAN'S WIFE'S PRAYER

The table's set, the meal's prepared, our guests will soon arrive,
My husband once more disappears with a hope of keeping a child alive.
While waiting at home alone, our plans having gone awry,
My first impulse is merely to sit right down and cry.
But soon again I realize the importance of my life,
When I agreed to take on the duties of being a fireman's wife.
While there are many drawbacks, I'll take them in my stride,
Knowing "My Daddy saved a life" our children can say with pride.
The gusting winds and raging flames may be his final fate,
But with God's help I can remain my fireman's faithful mate.

Author - Unknown

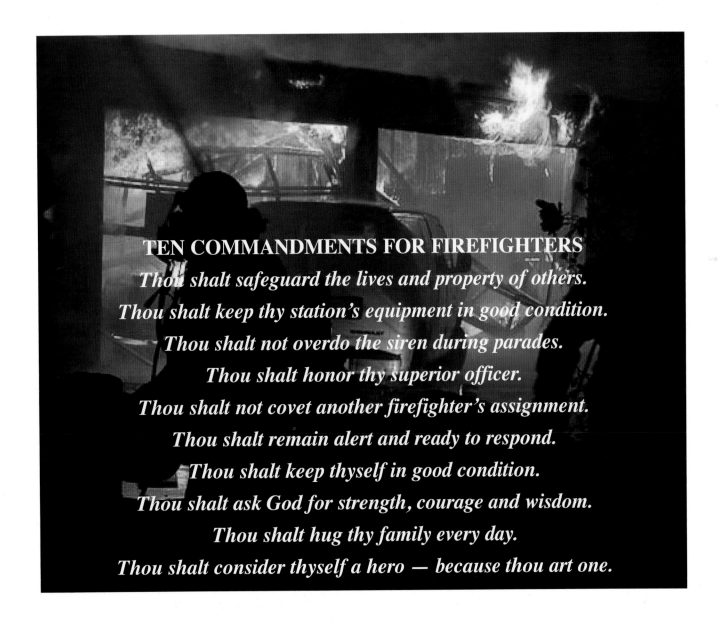

TEN COMMANDMENTS FOR FIREFIGHTERS

Thou shalt safeguard the lives and property of others.

Thou shalt keep thy station's equipment in good condition.

Thou shalt not overdo the siren during parades.

Thou shalt honor thy superior officer.

Thou shalt not covet another firefighter's assignment.

Thou shalt remain alert and ready to respond.

Thou shalt keep thyself in good condition.

Thou shalt ask God for strength, courage and wisdom.

Thou shalt hug thy family every day.

Thou shalt consider thyself a hero — because thou art one.

THE FIREFIGHTER'S COMMITTMENT

"I have no ambition in this world but one, and that is to be a firefighter. The position may, in the eyes of some, appear to be a lowly one; but we who know the work which the firefighter has to do believe that his is a noble calling.

There is an adage which says that, 'Nothing can be destroyed except by fire.' We strive to preserve from destruction the wealth of the world which is the product of the industry of men, necessary for the comfort of both the rich and the poor. We are defenders from fires of the art which has beautified the world, the product of the genius of men and the means of refinement of mankind. But, above all; our proudest endeavor is to save lives of men-the work of God Himself.

Under the impulse of such thoughts, the nobility of the occupation thrills us and stimulates us to deeds of daring, even at the supreme sacrifice. Such considerations may not strike the average mind, but they are sufficient to fill to the limit our ambition in life to make us serve the general purpose of human society."

Chief Edward F. Croker - FDNY circa 1910

THE LAST ALARM

My *father was a fireman, he drove a big red truck*
And when he'd go to work each day he'd say "Mother, wish me luck"
Then dad would not come home again until sometime the next day
But the thing that bothered me the most was the things some folks
would say
A fireman's life is easy, he eats and sleeps and plays,
and sometimes he won't fight a fire for many, many days
When I first heard these words
I was too young to
understand
But I knew when
people had trouble Dad
was there to lend a hand

Then my father went to work
one day and kissed us all
goodbye
but little did we realize that
night we all would cry
My father lost his life that
night when the floor gave way
below
And I wondered why he'd
risked his life for someone he
did not know
But now I truly realize the greatest gift a man can give
is to lay his life upon the line so that someone else might live
So as we go from day to day and pray to God above
Say a prayer for your local fireman
He may save the ones you love

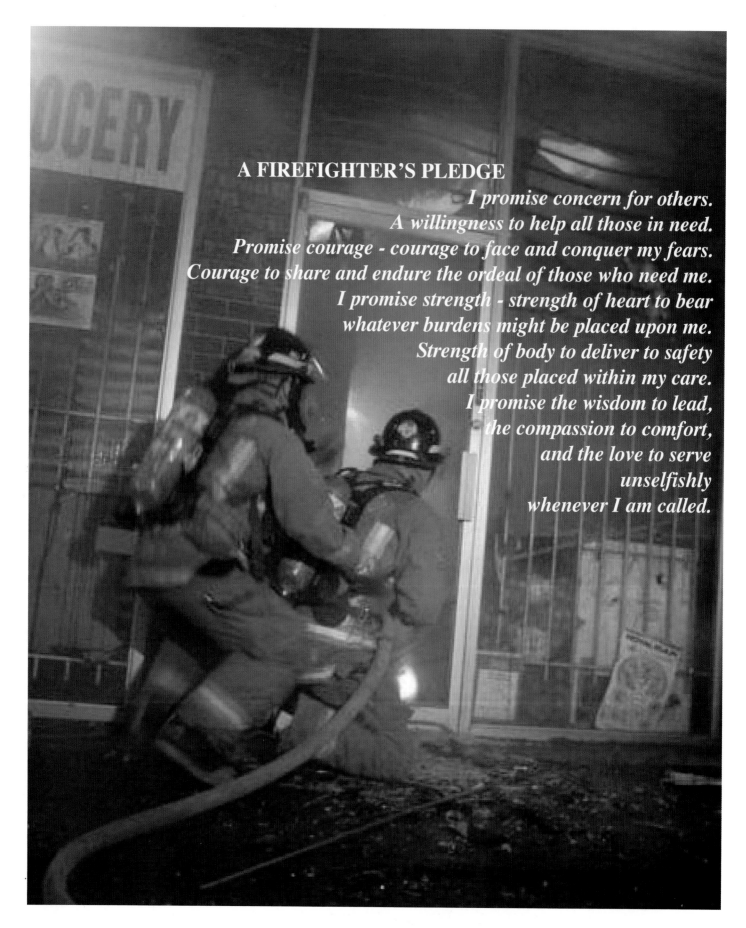

A FIREFIGHTER'S PLEDGE

I promise concern for others.
A willingness to help all those in need.
Promise courage - courage to face and conquer my fears.
Courage to share and endure the ordeal of those who need me.
I promise strength - strength of heart to bear
whatever burdens might be placed upon me.
Strength of body to deliver to safety
all those placed within my care.
I promise the wisdom to lead,
the compassion to comfort,
and the love to serve
unselfishly
whenever I am called.

Chapter II
Old Time Firefighter's Alphabet

A stands for Alarm, which shows folks the way to call up the firemen by night or by day.

B stands for the Bell we're so glad to hear, because then we know that help is quite near.

C is the fire Chief, in uniform blue, who tells all the others just what to do.

D is the Driver, who with reins in his hands, drives three horses abreast that obey his commands.

Lots & Lots of **FIRE TRUCKS & FIREFIGHTERS**

E is the Engine that gets up the steam, to pump up the water in such a big stream.

F stands for the Fire, that fills us with fright, when it breaks out in the dead of the night.

G is the Gong, on the engine-house walls, that sends off the men to where duty calls.

H stands for the Hose, and do not forget, that if it should burst you'll get very wet.

I the Insurance patrol, that usually brings appliances, many to safeguard our things.

J is the Jump to the life-saving net, an act of great courage that none can forget.

K is the Knowledge that gives men the power to fight smoke and flames for hour after hour.

L stands for Lantern, that burns with a glow, to light up dark places, where men have to go.

M is the Motor, the engine that's newest, to get to a fire in minutes the fewest.

N stands for the Nozzle, that they can't do without, when they turn on the water, to put the fire out.

O the Old time machine, of years long ago, that method of working appears rather slow.

P is the Pole, down which firemen scurry, instead of the stairs when they're in a big hurry.

Q stands for Quarters where all firemen stay, and await the alarm prepared for the fray.

R is the River Patrol, an engine that floats and puts out the fire on the docks and the boats.

S the Saving of lives, and for which they receive a small badge of honor, to wear on the sleeve.

T stands for the Truck, which as you know bears the ladders to reach those in danger upstairs.

U for the Uniform, that all firemen wear, respect it, because of the dangers they dare.

V is for Volunteers, who in times that are past, used to run with their engines and had to run fast.

W for the Watertower, which throws water so high that it seems as though it went up to the sky.

X stands for Xmas, and pray do not forget they are happy as children, with the presents they get.

Y is a Young American, who toots on the horn and thinks, the department, some day he'll adorn.

Z stands for the Zeal, which day after day in putting out fires, these brave men display. And now is the end, so "Good bye and good luck", are the parting words of good Father Tuck.

Chapter 12
Classic Fire House Traditions

THE MALTESE CROSS

The badge of a firefighter is the Maltese Cross. The Cross is a symbol of protection, a badge of honor, and its story is hundreds of years old. When a courageous band of crusaders known as the Knights of St. John fought the Saracens for possession of the Holy Land in the 13th Century, they encountered a new weapon unknown to European warriors. It was a simple, but a horrible device of war - The Saracen's weapon was fire.

As the crusaders advanced on the walls of the city, they were struck by glass bombs containing naphtha, a highly flammable liquid. When the area became saturated, the Saracens then hurled a flaming torch into their midst. Hundreds of the knights were burned alive; others risked their lives to save their brothers-in-arms from dying painful, fiery deaths. Thus, these men became our first firefighters and the first of a long list of courageous firefighters. Their heroic efforts were recognized by fellow crusaders who awarded each a badge of honor - a cross similar to the one firefighters wear today.

The Knights of St. John lived for close to four centuries on a little island in the Mediterranean Sea named Malta, hence the cross came to be known as the Maltese Cross. Today, the Maltese Cross means that firefighters, like Fireman Joe, wear this cross and are willing to lay down their lives for you – just as the crusaders sacrificed their lives for their fellow man so many years ago.

DALMATIAN - THE FIRE HOUSE DOG

How did the Dalmatian become the number one firefighting mascot in the United States and England? The Dalmatian has a strong muscular body and is able to run great distances without tiring. During the 17th, 18th and 19th centuries, most people traveled by horse or by carriage. The Dalmatians became a society dog, and were trained to run alongside women's carriages. They became known as Coach dogs or Ladies dogs. In fact, the term "coaching" refers to how the Dalmatian will take up position just off the side and toward the rear of a horse and run with them.

Through the years, Dalmatians worked closely with horses and their owners, sometimes even sleeping with the horses at night to protect the horses from being stolen. It is during the era of horse-drawn fire apparatus that the Dalmatian became forever tied with the Fire Service. Firehouse horses were required to spend many hours at a time at a fire scene or inside the firehouse waiting for a call. The Dalmatians became the horses' pets, and helped to keep them calm. The Dalmatian also became a guard dog, insuring that nothing was stolen from the apparatus during fire calls.

Today, in many large cities, the Dalmatian guards the fire truck while at the scene of fires and rescues, and has even been known to rescue trapped firefighters and victims. Overall, the Dalmatian is a brave and valiant dog. These traits make it an excellent mascot for the Fire Service.

FIREFIGHTER JOE'S FIREHOUSE RECIPES

Firehouse Sloppy Joes
Prep: 20 minutes
Cook: 20 to 30 minutes
Serves 8-10
INGREDIENTS:
5 lbs. Ground Beef
1 large onion (minced)
2 1/2 cups Ketchup
1/2 cup Mustard
3/4 cup Brown Sugar (dark)
5 tbsp. Lemon Juice
5 tbsp. Cider Vinegar
5 tbsp. Worchester Sauce
10 tbsp. water

DIRECTIONS:
Brown Ground beef and onions in large skillet, drain well. In a pan, add the rest of ingredients to make sauce, simmer on low heat. Add ground beef & onions to sauce, stir occasionally. Serve on hamburger buns. Great with Coleslaw & Fries for a quick dinner before or after that big blaze!

Firehouse Chili (Texas-style)
Prep: 10 minutes
Cook: 3 to 3-1/2 hours
Serves 8
INGREDIENTS:
6 lbs. lean beef, cut into 1/4-inch pieces
4 Tbsp. onion powder
2 tsp. garlic powder
2 can (16 oz.) tomato sauce
4 Tbsp. chili powder

Mix together:
8 Tbsp. chili powder
4 Tbsp. ground cumin
2 Tbsp. paprika
1/2tsp. ground oregano

1 tsp. cayenne pepper
1 tsp. ground white pepper
1 tsp. onion powder
2 Tbsp. garlic powder
1 tsp. salt

DIRECTIONS:
Sear meat in a large, heavy pot. Add onion powder and garlic powder, tomato sauce and 1/2 of mixed seasonings. Add water or beef broth to just cover meat. Stir and cook 2 to 3 hours, or until meat is nearly tender.

About 1/2 hour before completion, add remaining spices and continue cooking until meat is very tender. Add more salt if needed.

During cooking add additional water and/or beef broth to keep meat covered with gravy or a nice consistency (not too thick or thin).

Ginger-Glazed Miniature Firehouse Meat Loaves
Prep: 30 minutes
Cook: 60 minutes
Serves 12
INGREDIENTS:
2 small onions, minced
2 eggs
1 cup ketchup
2 tablespoons worcestershire sauce
2 teaspoons each: salt, freshly ground pepper
2 pounds ground beef chuck
1 pound ground pork

GLAZE:
1/2 cup ketchup
4 tablespoons brown sugar
2 teaspoon freshly ground ginger

DIRECTIONS:
Cook onions in a skillet over medium high heat about 5 minutes. Place eggs, ketchup, Worcestershire sauce, salt and pepper in a large bowl; beat until well blended. Stir in cooked onion and ground meats; blend well.

Put the mixture in small disposable bread loaf pans and put about 3 small holes in the bottom to ensure the grease can come out. Place the pans on a rack over a cookie sheet.

Bake @ 375 degrees for about an hour - after 45 minutes put the glaze on and bake another 15 minutes...make sure the grease is drained - hopefully your holes are big enough...if not - drain before glaze is put on.

Cola Chicken

Prep: 30 minutes
Cook: 70 minutes
Serves 12 to 16
INGREDIENTS:
4 chickens, cut into 32 pieces
40 ounces cola drink (5 cups)
4 cups ketchup
6 tablespoons dried mustard powder
Salt & black pepper to taste

DIRECTIONS:
Salt & pepper chicken and place in skillet or pan depending on quantity. Make mixture of cola, ketchup, and mustard powder. Pour mixture over chicken. Cover and simmer 45 to 60 minutes before removing cover to let sauce thicken.

Firehouse Fruit Dump Cobbler

Prep: 20 minutes
Cook: 60 minutes
Serves 8
INGREDIENTS:
1 stick of butter
2 cups of sugar
1 1/2 cups of flour
2 tsp salt
2 tsp baking powder
1 1/2 cups of milk
2 cans pie filling (apple, strawberry, blueberry, cherry or peach)

DIRECTIONS:
Melt butter in 8" x 16" pan. Mix all ingredients, except pie filling in a bowl. Pour mix into pan with melted butter. Add pie filling and spread evenly throughout mix, bake at 350 degrees for approximately 1 hour.

Firehouse Sausage Gravy
Prep: 10 minutes
Cook: 20 minutes

INGREDIENTS:
3 lbs. of Good Bulk Sausage
2 cans Evaporated Milk
4 Tablespoons of Flour
Salt, Pepper, Water to Taste
Serves 8

DIRECTIONS:
Brown sausage in large skillet. Pour off grease, reserving four tbsp of grease. On medium heat, add flour, stir and cook for two minutes with sausage. Add Milk, Pepper, 16 to 20 oz of water, then stir mixture until a thick gravy is form.

Gravy can be thickened or thinned by using more/less water. Salt to taste. Enjoy over hot buttermilk biscuits.

Chapter 13
History of Fire Trucks & Firefighting

The history of firefighters and firefighting is thousands of years old. Archaeological evidence shows that ancient Egyptians used hand-operated wooden water pumps in 200 BCE (Before Common Era.) Ancient Rome had a paid force of more than 7000 firefighters. The Dutch used leather hoses in the 17th Century.

Long before America fought fires with snorkels, hook and ladder trucks, and pumpers, it used the simple bucket brigade. In the eighteenth-century colonies, neighbors would form lines, carrying buckets of water by hand from local streams and rivers to the blazing wooden home of an unfortunate citizen.

Statesman Benjamin Franklin organized one of the first fire departments in America, serving Philadelphia in the mid-1700's.

Lots & Lots of FIRE TRUCKS & FIREFIGHTERS

As cities began to sprout up in America, the number of public and business buildings grew. Fires in these structures were costly, in terms of inventory and furniture, as well as lives. Insurance companies began "fire patrols" or "insurance patrols" to salvage goods and materials from these fires. Independent from fire departments, these patrols prevented water and fire damage to property during and after the fires. Only the largest of American metropolitan areas had insurance patrols – by the mid-1800's, 19 cities had them. By the early 1930's, insurance patrols began to disappear, as fire departments became more sophisticated. Firefighting embraced the concept of "fire prevention."

By the middle 1800's, America fought fires with horse-drawn pumpers – using steam engines to draw water from various sources, delivering pressurized water via leather and rubber fire hoses. As public and private buildings began to add stories and levels, firefighters added ladders to their equipment following the Civil War.

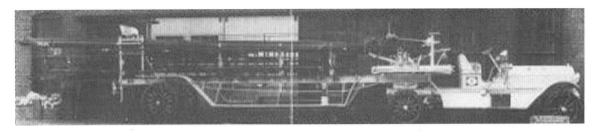

Early into the 20th Century, firefighting was revolutionized with the invention of the motorized fire truck – one motor powered the vehicle, while another drove the water pumps. In no time, sirens were installed on fire trucks, providing the public with a warning of the approaching rescue equipment.

Aerial ladders, capable of rotating and extending to the upper floors of burning buildings, started showing up on fire trucks in the 1910's. World War II added other firefighting developments, such as airport crash equipment and improved wireless communications.

Rescue trucks with extension buckets appeared in the late 1950's, with the eventual introduction of the snorkel pumping unit in the 1960's.

Up to now, the sight of a shiny red fire truck, speeding to a fire, was familiar across America. But in the mid-1970's, "safety green" became the rage, shocking many traditionalists – both firefighters and firewatchers.

Today, most fire trucks have returned to the long-established red color – and have become more flexible, providing rescue and emergency service for hazardous materials and paramedic needs, as well as continuing to douse the fires of America.

Lots & Lots of **FIRE TRUCKS & FIREFIGHTERS**

Chapter 14
Antique Fire Trucks

Fire museums like the Aurora Regional Fire Museum in Aurora, Illinois pay tribute to the brave firefighters of America, as well as the sturdy antique vehicles that helped them do their job.

1850s Button Hand Pumper
This hand pumper was made by Button and Company of Waterford, New York sometime in the 1850s.

Lots & Lots of **FIRE TRUCKS & FIREFIGHTERS**

1907 Ahrens

The Ahrens Manufacturing Company is a direct descendant of the first successful steam fire engine manufacturer in America. The Ahrens company (in all its incarnations) produced nearly one-thousand steam fire engines between 1852 and 1916.

1916 Jeffery

This engine is typical of those utilized by smaller communities in the early 1900's.

The chassis was manufactured by the Jeffrey Motor Company and then delivered to Kenosha, Wisconsin, where the hose body was installed by the Pirsch Fire Apparatus Company.

This engine was merely a hose wagon. Having no chemical tanks or pump, the firefighters would use it to transport their hose to the fire scene where it would be attached directly to a fire hydrant.

1918 American LaFrance

Delivered in 1918, this American LaFrance pumper served the small community of LaSalle, Illinois for over forty years. Early American LaFrance engines such as this one were often called the Ford Model "Ts" of the fire service. They were common, relatively affordable, and very reliable.

1921 Stutz

Like most fire engines of the day, the Stutz was considered a triple combination - containing a pump, hose, and chemical tanks. It was assigned to Company Number 3.

In 1943, Peter Pirsch Fire Apparatus Company completely reconditioned the Stutz, adding a new Waukesha engine, replacing the solid rubber tires, and both widening and strengthening the frame.

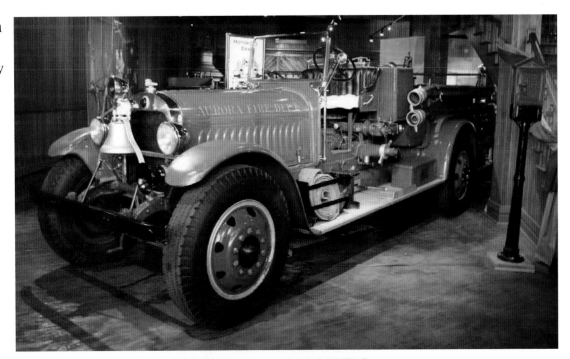

Lots & Lots of **FIRE TRUCKS & FIREFIGHTERS**

1934 Pirsch Service Truck

The Pirsch Quadruple Combination Service Truck is technically referred to as a "Quad" because of the truck's pump, water tank, hose body, and ladder carrying ability. The combination of these four functions, and some additional rescue and lighting equipment, made this truck extremely versatile.

1942 America LaFrance

The 500 series American LaFrance featured a pump mounted in front of the cab and behind the motor. The pump's control panel was located on the passenger side of the engine, a "safety feature" briefly tried and abandoned by American LaFrance in the 1940's.

1945 America LaFrance

While World War II had just ended, the repercussions of the war had not. During the war years, all metal and manufacturing were standardized and strictly rationed. Even makers of fire apparatus were not exempt. Civilian orders for fire trucks were prioritized and those that were made had a more spartan appearance. Front bumpers and grills, once brightly chrome plated, were merely painted silver or gray. Fancy lettering, pin striping, and gold leafing also all but disappeared. The American LaFrance Company produced many of these Type 500 pumpers through the war years and just after.

1948 America LaFrance

Delivered in 1948, this American LaFrance "700 series" pumper served as Engine No. 3 in the community of Batavia, Illinois for over forty years.

Typical of most fire apparatus made after World War II, the 700 series sported a new design that placed the cab in front of the motor. This eliminated the long nose from the front of the engine and provided for better visibility and maneuverability. The new cab also allowed five firefighters to sit down and ride inside. This was much safer than in previous models, where the firefighters would ride to the fire while standing on the back running board and hang on for dear life.

The new 700 series cab was a huge success for the American LaFrance Fire Engine Company. Over three thousand 700 series pumpers, ladder trucks, rescue squads, and even airport crash vehicles were manufactured between 1947 and 1956. The engine's popularity, and its distinctive front end, make it the quintessential American fire engine.

Chapter 15
Greatest Fires in History

Ever since earliest man struck two pieces of flint together to create a spark, fire has been one of the most important elements in the development of the human race. Fire is responsible for providing light, melting steel, cooking food, warming cold rooms, creating steam, and much more. But, when fire gets out of control it can be devastating. Because space does not allow the listing of all the disastrous fires in history, six of the most famous are recapped here. For further information on the greatest fires in history, see the timeline in Chapter 16.

ROME BURNS IN 64 A.D.

The night of July 19, 64 A.D. was hot when a fire broke out among the shops surrounding the Circus Maximus, Rome's gigantic chariot stadium. In itself, this was not an unusual occurrence, since the sweltering summer heat started fires around Rome on a regular basis, particularly in the poorer sections of the city. The flames raged for six days before calming down. Then the fire reignited and burned for another three days. Although it is not known how many people died in the fire, the population of Rome at the time was two million. When the smoke cleared after the fire, ten of Rome's fourteen districts were in shambles – almost two-thirds of the city had been destroyed. Theory has it that the Emperor of the time, Nero, started the fire so that sections of the city would be leveled and allow him the opportunity to re-build the city in glorious fashion under his guidance and to his specifications. Legend also says that Nero "fiddled" while Rome burned. This is impossible, as the violin was not even invented until the mid-1500s. In actuality, the Roman emperor opened his palace to those who were left homeless by the disaster.

THE GREAT CHICAGO FIRE

The Great Chicago fire is probably the most famous fire that occurred within the past hundred years or so. This fire started on the evening of Sunday, October 8, 1871 at around 9 PM. The best-known story of the fire is that it was started by a cow's kicking over a lantern in the barn owned by Patrick and Catherine O'Leary at 137 DeKoven Street on Chicago's West Side. However, it is said that a reporter for a local newspaper created the cow story because he thought it would be "colorful reading."

Other accounts of the fire's origin include that it actually began when Daniel "Pegleg" Sullivan, who first reported the fire, ignited some hay in the barn while trying to steal some milk. Another story suggests that someone may have started the fire during a craps game. An alternative theory, first suggested in 1882, is that the Great Chicago Fire was actually caused by a meteor shower when Biela's Comet broke up over the Midwest and rained down on the city and surrounding areas of the Midwest. Eyewitness reports include sightings of "balls of fire" falling from the sky with blue flames. Still, another local legend has it that the fire was started by boys sneakily smoking pipes in a haystack.

Whatever the cause, once the fire started, it spread quickly through the closely packed wood buildings filled with fuel for oil lamps and barns full of hay and straw. It raced along sidewalks made of wood and through the lumber and coal yards along the river. Fueled by a strong northeasterly wind, the fire spread over 34 blocks, destroying everything in its path.

Although its true origin will probably never be known, it is known that it was a devastating fire that destroyed more than 17,000 structures – and destroyed over 2000 acres in 27 hours. Approximately 300 people lost their lives in this fire and 100,000 were left homeless. The population of Chicago at that time was approximately 340,000. Rainfall, which started about midnight on Monday, and diminishing winds helped extinguish the blaze. It was eventually determined that the fire destroyed an area about four miles long by ¾ mile wide.

Chicagoans quickly rebuilt their beloved "Windy City" and by 1875, little evidence of the disaster remained. Today, the Chicago Water Tower (made of stone) remains as the unofficial memorial to the fire's destructive power.

THE GREAT FIRE OF LONDON

This famous fire began in a baker's shop 1n 1666 and lasted for several days. Surprisingly, the Great London Fire has no reported death toll. However, it destroyed more than 13,000 structures.

London was also a city largely built of wood, another stack of kindling waiting to burn. When the city was rebuilt, builders used brick and stone to prevent a disaster of such proportions from ever happening again.

The Great Fire of London began on the night of Sunday , September 2, 1666, as a small fire on Pudding Lane, in the bakeshop of Thomas Farynor, baker to King Charles II. At one o'clock in the morning, a servant woke to find the house on fire, and the baker and his family escaped. The fire raged for three more days and finally died out on Wednesday, September 5.

Just like Chicago, most of the houses in London at the time were made of wood and pitch and once the fire started it easily spread to surrounding areas. Strong winds blew that night and sent sparks flying everywhere, igniting everything in the fire's path. The volunteer firefighting brigades had little or no success in dousing the fire with their buckets of water from the river and by eight o'clock in the morning, the fire had spread halfway across London Bridge.

The standard procedure to stop a fire from spreading in those days had always been to destroy the houses in

Lots & Lots of FIRE TRUCKS & FIREFIGHTERS

the path of the flames, creating what's known as "fire-breaks," to keep the fire from getting any more fuel. The problem in London at the time was the indecisiveness of Lord Mayor Bludworth to destroy any property for fear of the cost of rebuilding.

Although the loss of life was minimal (probably because there were few records of the poor living in London at that time), the amount of the property loss was staggering. Some 430 acres, almost eighty percent of the core city was destroyed, including approximately 13,000 houses, 89 churches, 52 Guild Halls and St. Paul's Cathedral. It is estimated that 70,000 of the city's 80,000 population were left homeless. A monument to the Great Fire still stands today at the site of the bakery which started it all, on a street now named Monument Street.

THE SAN FRANCISCO EARTHQUAKE

Not all fires are started by human negligence. The great San Francisco earthquake that hit the city and the coast of Northern California on the morning of Wednesday, April 18, 1906 caused not only damage from the collapse of buildings, but also tremendous devastation from the subsequent fires that erupted in the wake of the quake. The earthquake and resulting fire are to be remembered as one of the worst natural disasters in the history of the United States, right alongside Hurricane Katrina in 2005.

Many of the fires were caused by stoves and lamps that were overturned from the earthquake. The city's water mains burst from the quake, making it nearly impossible for firefighters to get any water to fight the fires that sprung up all over the city. Gas mains erupted where electrical wires crossed their paths. As a result, the fire lasted for three days until firefighters dynamited entire blocks of the city to prevent the spread of the fire; much like the tactics taken in the Great Fire of London.

Between 225,000 and 300,000 people were left homeless out of a population of approximately 410,000. The earthquake was the first natural disaster of its kind to be documented by photographs and movie film. The overall cost of the damage from the earthquake was estimated to be around $400 million in 1906 dollars and over 3,000 inhabitants lost their lives. Close to 300,000 buildings were destroyed by either fire or the quake.

GREAT BOSTON FIRE OF 1872

The Great Boston Fire of 1872 was Boston's largest city fire and still one of the most costly fire-related property losses in American history. The disaster began at 7:20 p.m. on November 9, in the basement of

a commercial warehouse at 83 - 87 Summer Street in Boston – possibly the act of an arsonist or a landlord looking to recoup insurance monies. The fire lasted about 12 hours and in the final analysis, destroyed about 65 acres of Boston's downtown area, including 776 buildings, much of the financial district and caused $73.5 million in damage. At least 20 people are known to have died in the fire.

Many factors contributed to Boston's Great Fire including faulty construction practices and poorly enforced building codes. Flying embers and cinders jumped from building to building, as many were made of wood known as French Mansard roofs, common in those days in Boston. Boston's city infrastructure was shoddy with old water pipes with low pressure and non-standard or insufficient hydrants. Steam engine pumpers were not able to draw enough water to put out the blaze. And gas lines used to feed lights exploded and made the fire worsen.

As was the case in all the disasters noted here, Boston rebuilt itself into the beautifully historic city it once was.

9/11

At 8:46 on the morning of September 11, 2001, the United States became a nation under siege.

An airliner traveling at hundreds of miles per hour and carrying some 10,000 gallons of jet fuel plowed into the North Tower of the World Trade Center in Lower Manhattan. At 9:03, a second airliner hit the South Tower. Fire and smoke billowed upward. Steel, glass, ash, and bodies fell below. The Twin Towers, where up to 50,000 people worked each day, both collapsed less than 90 minutes later.

At 9:37 that same morning, a third airliner slammed into the western

Lots & Lots of FIRE TRUCKS & FIREFIGHTERS

face of the Pentagon. At 10:03, a fourth airliner crashed in a field in southern Pennsylvania. It had been aimed at the United States Capitol or the White House, and was forced down by heroic passengers armed with the knowledge that America was under attack.

More than 2,600 people died at the World Trade Center; 125 died at the Pentagon; 256 died on the four planes. Among the fatalities were 343 brave New York City firefighters and 60 NYC and Port Authority police officers. The death toll from 9/11 surpassed that at Pearl Harbor in December 1941.

The plot was carried out by nineteen young Arabs acting at the behest of Islamist extremists headquartered in distant Afghanistan. Some had been in the United States for more than a year, mixing in with the rest of the population. Although four were trained as pilots, most were not well-educated. In most cases, the terrorists spoke English poorly, some hardly at all. In groups of four or five, carrying with them only small knives, box cutters, and cans of Mace or pepper spray, they had hijacked the four planes and turned them into deadly guided missiles against America.

Lots & Lots of FIRE TRUCKS & FIREFIGHTERS

Chapter 16
Firefighting Timeline

Ever since lighting struck a dry tree and man discovered how to strike two pieces of flint together, fire has been one of the most important elements in the formation of life on earth. Throughout time, no matter how far along man has advanced technologically or socially, fire has always been an integral part of our lives. Through the centuries it has cooked our food, heated our homes, guided us in the night, and been the focal point of religious and communal ceremonies. It has fueled the shops and factories that have allowed us to create the tools and weapons necessary for survival – from hunting spears and knives to steel for cars and spaceships. In this timeline, you will find some of the more important points of interest in man's encounters with fire, as well as some general historic events for reference.

50 B.C.
* The library of Alexandria possibly burned accidentally during a battle.

Vesuvius erupts in 79 A.D.

64 A.D.
* July 19 - Rome burns for six days destroying almost two-thirds of the city. One theory claims the fire was started by Emperor Nero so he could re-build the city to his liking.

79
* August 24 - the Roman city of Pompeii (near what is now Naples, Italy) is ruined during a catastrophic eruption of the Mount Vesuvius volcano. The volcano buried the city under many feet of ash and it was lost for 1600 years before its rediscovery in 1748 by local residents.

1068
* William the Conqueror initiates curfew bells to be rung at seven in the evening to alert citizens to cover all fires and extinguish lights.

1204
* City of Constantinople (now Istanbul,) capitol of the Roman Empire, is burned three times during the Fourth Crusade.

1347
* Chimneys become commonplace in Venice, Italy.

1368
* Chimneys brought to use in Rome by Francesco de Carrao, Lord of Padura.

1607
* First settlement in the "new world" founded in Jamestown.

1609
* January 7 - Jamestown, VA settlement destroyed by fire. All provisions are lost and many die of hunger and exposure to the harsh winter weather.

1613
* Dutch trading ship Tiger burns in New York Harbor, forcing her crew to be the first settlers on Manhattan.

1620
* Pilgrims land at Plymouth Rock.

1621
* Brick chimney law put into effect in England.

1623
* November 1 - Fire destroys seven dwellings at Plymouth and nearly ends settlement.

1631
* March 16 - The first fire in Boston occurs, due to the imperfect claying of a chimney in which two buildings were destroyed.

1648
* Peter Stuyvesant, Governor of New Amsterdam, appoints four fire wardens to perform inspections of chimneys. Fire prevention ordinances are passed and fines are imposed to purchase and maintain fire buckets, hooks and ladders.

1653

* January 14 - First of Boston's "great" fires destroys one-third of the town.

1654

* Joseph Jynks of Saugus, MA, builds first American fire "enjyne."

1664

* British take over New Amsterdam and the town is renamed "New York."

1666

* September 2 - Great Fire of London, England. On the night of Sunday, September 2, fire breaks out in a baker's shop and burns for several days, destroying more than 13,000 structures.

1676

* November 27 - Fire in Boston destroys large part of North End, including Increase Mather's church.

1679

* Boston imports fire engines from England.

Great Fire of London

1711

* "Towne House Fire" in Boston.

1718

* Mutual Fire Society organized in Boston by progressive citizens. This first volunteer fire company in America only battled fire among its own members homes.

1728

* Copenhagen, Denmark fire burns two-fifths of the city over three days, leaving 3,650 families homeless.

1731

* Newsham fire engines arrive in New York from London.

1736

* Benjamin Franklin establishes the Union Fire Company, the first fire organization in Philadelphia and one of the first in America to fight fires for the public good.

1740

* November 18 - Fire in Charleston, SC. All houses and buildings from Broad and Church Streets to East Battery are burned down.

1741

* March 18 - Fort George on lower end of Manhattan burns. New Yorkers incited to rise against so-called "Negro Plot."

1743

* First successful pumping engine built in America, by Thomas Lote of New York.

1752

* Philadelphia Contributionship started; the first successful fire-insurance company in America.

British burn New York City

1770

* March 5 - Boston Massacre. British troops opened fire on a mob of colonists. The shooting may have started when a wayward cry of "fire" was given — a cry intended to sound the town's church and fire bells as an alarm.

1775

* April 19 - Paul Revere's famous ride.
* June 17 - Battle of Bunker Hill. Redcoats set fire to 380 dwellings in Charlestown, MA.

1776

* July 4 - Declaration of Independence.
* September 21 - New York City burned. Continental Army believed to have set the fires that destroyed 493 buildings to oust British occupation forces.

1785

* A powerful new, American designed, "Gooseneck" style fire engine is introduced.

1788

* March 21 - New Orleans destroyed by fire on Good Friday. The fire begins by a curtain blowing over an open candle. Over 900 buildings (seven-eighths of the town) burned.

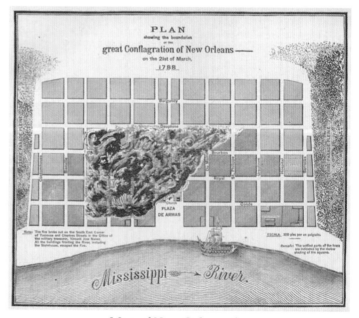

Map of New Orleans fire

1789
* George Washington becomes first President of the United States.

1791
* Journals recording fire-company duty and activities first used.
* First double-deck/end stroke hand engine built in Philadelphia.

1792
* Insurance Company of North America is formed.

1796
* December 9 - "Coffee House Slip" Fire in New York.

1797
* Newark, NJ organizes a fire company and purchases small hand-engine.

1800
* English inventor John Carry, designs the first crude automatic sprinkler, but it goes undeveloped for a long period.

1803
* Fort Dearborn, Chicago founded.
* Volunteer fire department established in Cincinnati, OH.
* Wooden hydrants installed in Philadelphia.

1805
* June 11 - Detroit, MI destroyed by fire.

1806
* In the aftermath of a major fire in Philadelphia, hydrant inspections begin.

1807
* Early fire prevention activity in Washington, DC resulted in all chimneys being cleaned.

1808
* Fire Bucket Company formed in Cincinnati, OH.
* New York City gets first hydrant attached to underground water main.
* A new concept in fire fighting is introduced, leather fire hose seamed by copper rivets.

1809
* The first fireboat (Engine 42 of New York) is hand-rowed and hand-pumped.

1811
* Philadelphia diverted water from storage tanks in the street for use in fighting fires.
* Philadelphia Hose Co. formed.
* May 31 - Fire destroys 250 buildings in Newburyport, MA.
* Theatre Fire claims 72 victims in Richmond, VA.

1812 to 1814
* The war with England brings major conflagrations: Capitol Building, State Department, Treasury Building, and Government Arsenal - all are
destroyed by fire.
* "Fire rafts" (burning ships set adrift) are used to threaten and destroy the enemy.

1814
* The White House in Washington, D.C. burned by the British.

1816
* Richmond, VA organizes the Richmond Fire Society for the purpose rendering mutual aid.

1819
* Philadelphia organizes a special fire patrol group to perform salvage work.

White House burns in 1814

1820
* January 11 - Fire destroys 463 buildings, mostly dwellings in Savannah, GA.

1821
* A volunteer fire company is organized in St. Louis, MO.

1827
* English chemist John Walter invents the friction match containing phosphorus sulfate.

1825
* Erie Canal opens.

1829
* George Braithwaite builds first fire engine using steam to pump water.

1830
* B&0 Railroad, (the first in America), makes successful run.
* Fire protection improvements in Richmond, VA includes a water supply system reservoir, water pump hose and private hydrants.

1832
* Horses begin pulling engines after Asiatic cholera plague strikes firemen.
* Sectional ladders used by John Braidwood of London.

Great Fire of New York City

1835
* December 16 - Great Fire of New York City. Over 650 buildings, including most of the Wall Street financial area are destroyed and result in $20-40 million property loss. Following the conflagration, private patrols are appointed to cover the city in event of second fire.

1837
* Depression and panic sweep America.
* June 10 - Broad Street Riot in Boston. Firemen fight Irishmen all day.
* Milwaukee, WI forms its first volunteer fire company.

1840
* Henry R. Worthington invents an independent, direct-acting steam pump.

1841
* Paul Hodge builds the first steam fire engine in America. He is scorned by the volunteer firefighters of New York.

1844
* Samuel F. B. Morse invents the telegraph.

1845
* Dr. William F. Channing of Boston invents the fire-alarm telegraph.
* April 10 - Great Fire of Pittsburgh; 982 buildings burned, mostly dwellings.
* Potato famine in Ireland. Irish come to America in great numbers.

1846
* July 13 - Fire in Nantucket, MA. With 300 buildings destroyed, the town's whaling supremacy comes to an end.

Fire in Nantucket, MA.

1848
* August 17 - Fire in Albany, NY, destroys 600 buildings.

1849
* California Gold Rush begins.
* San Francisco. A conflagration caused by arson results in $12 million in property damage. Following the fire, vigilante groups are organized to patrol the city and watch for more arsonists.
* May 17 - A conflagration that began on the ship "White Cloud" destroys twenty-six river boats, 418 buildings, and kills twenty in St. Louis, MO. First U.S. firefighter killed in the line of duty.

1850
* Fire destroys 400 buildings in Philadelphia and kills thirty-nine people.

1851
* May 4 - The worst of six big incendiary fires that sweep San Francisco between December, 1849, and June, 1851. This one almost destroys the entire city.

Riverside fire in St. Louis, MO.

1852
* First fire-alarm telegraph central office and street box system inaugurated in Boston.
* Patent issued for first sprinkler-perforated pipe system. This is the first recognized installation of fire protection equipment.

1853
* Latta Brothers steam fire engine, "Uncle Joe Ross," revolutionizes firefighting. Cincinnati becomes the first American city to replace volunteers with the horse-drawn steam fire engine, and to form a paid fire department.
* December 27 - Great Republic, biggest clipper ship ever built, burns in New York on the eve of her maiden voyage.

NYC's Crystal Palace aflame

1854
* Jennings Building fire causes four deaths in New York City.

1857
* St. Louis forms the second fully paid steam fire department in America.
* Crystal Palace, New York City, burns to the ground. Being constructed almost entirely of iron and glass, with only a little wood near its base, the

Crystal Palace was called "fireproof" at the time of its construction, however it faced the same ironic fate as that of the "unsinkable" Titanic. The enormous building burns to the ground in less than half-an-hour.

1859
* Baltimore, MD establishes its first paid fire department.

1860
* January 10 - Pemberton Mills Fire in Lawrence, MA.; 115 killed.
* February 2 - Elm Street Tenement Fire in New York City; 200 killed. Laws requiring fire escapes are passed as a result of this fire.

1861
* Milwaukee, WI establishes a paid fire company.
* Washington, DC fire department becomes a fully paid organization and installs a fire alarm telegraph.
* April 12 - Fort Sumter is attacked and the Civil War begins.
* New York City firefighters organize the first Fire Zouaves regiments (part-firefighter and part-soldier) and leave for the battlefront.
* December 11 - Most of Charleston, SC is destroyed by fire because of the Civil War.

1863
* July 1 - 3 - Battle of Gettysburg.
* July - Draft riots occur in many United States cities.
* New York City institutes a paid fire department.
* Iglesia de la Compania de Jesus fire in Santiago, Chile kills over 2000.

1864
* November 8 – the "Southern Conspiracy" to burn New York City.
* The city of Atlanta is burned after evacuation by General Sherman during the Civil War.

Fires of the Civil War destroy Charleston, SC.

1865
* General Robert E. Lee surrenders to General Ulysses S. Grant at Appomatox Courthouse, VA.
* April 14 - President Abraham Lincoln assassinated.
* April 27 - S.S. Sultana explodes in Mississippi River; 1450 killed.

1866
* Atlantic Cable successfully laid.
* July 4 - Great Fire in Portland, ME. Firecracker starts blaze that destroys 1500 buildings.

1869
* Railroad spans America, coast to coast.

1870
* "Boss" Tweed era of corruption in New York at its height.
* Philadelphia, PA., gets a paid fire department.
* Daniel Hayes, a San Francisco fireman, develops the first successful aerial ladder truck.

Great Fire in Portland, ME.

1871
* First volunteer firefighting unit organized in Los Angeles, CA.
* Rubber-lined, cotton-jacketed, fire hose begins to replace the riveted leather hose.

Forest fires in Peshtigo, WI.

* October 8 - The Great Chicago Fire. Approximately 18,000 buildings burned, over 200 lives lost. Help comes from eight states to battle the two-day conflagration.
* Also on October 8, forest fires destroy the town of Peshtigo, WI, killing 1500 – 2000 and raging on through parts of Michigan.

1872
* November 9 – The Great Fire of Boston.
* Great Fire of Boston destroys 776 buildings and one square mile of the business district.
* More than seventy insurance companies go bankrupt as a result of the Great Fire of Boston. The companies that survive form the National Board of Underwriters and establish safeguards for insurance companies to follow.

1873
* Quick-hitch horse collar and harnesses invented by Charles Berry a fireman in Cambridge, MA.
* Suspended harness invented by firemen in St. Joseph, MO.
* First sliding poles, (made of wood,) are installed in some New York engine houses.

1874
* Automatic sprinklers introduced.
* First high-pressure water system for fighting fires installed in Rochester, NY.

1876
* Telephone invented by Alexander Graham Bell.
* Major league baseball is organized.
* December 5 - Brooklyn Theater Fire; 295 killed.

1879
* Thomas Edison invents the incandescent lamp.

1880
* Frederick Grinnell improves upon the automatic sprinkler. Insurance companies cut rates to businesses installing Grinnell sprinklers.

1881
* Ring Theater fire claims 850 victims in Vienna.

1887
* May 25 - Paris Opera fire kills 200.

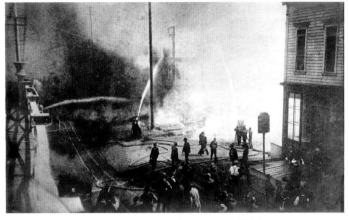
The Great Seattle Fire of 1889

1889
* Henry Ford builds his first car.
* May 31 - The Johnstown Flood, 2200 people killed in PA.
* June 6 - Fire destroys thirty-one blocks in center of city and along the waterfront in Seattle, WA.

1894
* Moving-picture machine invented by Edison.
* The Great Fire of Shanghai, where over 1000 buildings are destroyed.

1895
* February 14 - Fire at Lynn, MA., destroys 300 buildings in center of city, mostly factories.

1897
* Klondike Gold Rush in Yukon Territory, Canada.

1898
* Spanish-American War breaks out after warship U.S.S. Maine explodes in Havana, Cuba harbor.

U.S.S. Maine arrives in Havana harbor

Lots & Lots of FIRE TRUCKS & FIREFIGHTERS

1900
* June 30 - Fire sweeps through the Hoboken, NJ water front; 400 killed.

Jacksonville, FL. fire in 1901

1901
* May 3 - Fire destroys 1700 buildings in Jacksonville, FL, claims 7 victims.
* Marconi transmits the first wireless message across the Atlantic.
* President Wm. McKinley is assassinated and Theodore Roosevelt becomes 25th President.

1902
* Wright Brothers make first airplane flight.
* February 8 - Fire burns 525 buildings in Paterson, NJ.

1903
* December 30 – Iroquois Theater fire in Chicago results in 602 deaths and 250 injuries.

1904
* Successful firefighting breathing apparatus invented, but not adopted for a number of years.
* February 7 - Great Fire of Baltimore engulfs eighty downtown blocks, with 1343 buildings burned. The Baltimore fire raises national atten-

Iroquois Theater in Chicago

tion for the need to standardize fire hose couplings and screw threads.
* June 15 – The General Slocum, an excursion steamer with combustibles on board, catches on fire while cruising in New York's East River. Close to 1030 lives are lost, mostly children. This fire leads to the inspection of ships in New York Harbor.

General Slocum afire in the East River

1906

* April 18 - The San Francisco earthquake and fire destroys 28,000 buildings, with over 3000 deaths and $400 million in property damage.

1907

* Gasoline-powered motors and pumps begin to appear in the fire service.
* Underwriters Laboratories initiates its factory inspection service and begins to issue labels for "approved devices."
* Invention of first pumper with a single engine to do both driving and pumping.

1908

* March 4 – Fire at the Lakeview Grammar School in Collinwood, OH. Tragically, 175 children and one teacher are killed.
* April 12 - Conflagration in Chelsea, MA, burns 3500 buildings and kills eighteen.

School fire in Collinwood, OH.

1910

* January 28 - Fire of unknown origin starts in the Nelson Morris Co. Packing Plant, Kansas City, KS and causes a loss estimated at half a million dollars before it is brought under control.
* December 22 – Chicago's Union Stockyards and Transit Company erupts in a horrific blaze that rages for 24 hours and takes the lives of 21 firefighters. This fire ranks as the third largest in U.S History behind the 9-11 terrorist attacks and the 1947 Texas City disaster in terms of firefighter's lives lost.
* New York City fire, Grand Central terminal yard.
* Transport of hazardous materials is quickly becoming a great threat in American commerce.

1911

* March 25 – Largest industrial fire of the time at the Triangle Shirtwaist factory in New York City.

Fire at NYC's Triangle Shirtwaist Factory

Lots & Lots of FIRE TRUCKS & FIREFIGHTERS

Over 150 people killed, mostly young women. This fire arouses the public and labor against sweat shops and child labor.
* New York City creates the Committee on Safety, which leads directly to the Safety to Life Committee of the National Fire Protection Association, (the NFPA).

1912
* Equitable Building fire in New York City.
* The Titanic hits iceberg and sinks - 1513 lives are lost.

1913
* Fire destroys 518 buildings in Hot Springs, AR.
* Binghamton Clothing Factory fire results in new standard for building exits - 35 people lose their lives.
* Single-driving and pumping engine developed to efficiency.

1914
* June 25 - 1600 buildings are destroyed when fire sweeps through Salem, MA.
* The Panama Canal is opened.
* World War I begins in Europe.

1915
• Telephone service from New York to San Francisco is initiated.
• The S.S. Lusitania is sunk.

1916
* March 21 - Fire burns 1440 buildings, nearly the entire town of Paris, TX.

Salem, MA. fire in 1914

* March 22 - Fire in Nashville, TN burns 648 buildings, mostly dwellings.
* March 22 - More than 680 buildings burn in downtown Augusta, GA.
* July 30 - "Black Tom Pier" fire and explosion in New Jersey.

1917
* Ammunition storage explosion kills 1,500 in Halifax, Nova Scotia.
* Eddystone Ammunition Corporation explosion in Eddystone, PA - 133 lose their lives.
* April 6 - United States enters World War I.

Damage at the Black Tom Pier, NJ.

* May 21 - Simultaneous fires destroy 1938 buildings over 73 blocks in Atlanta, GA.

1918
* International Association of Firefighters Union organized.
* October forest fires in Minnesota sweep through fifteen townships, destroying property and killing 559.
* November 11 - Armistice is signed, World War I ends.

1919
* Two-platoon system begins in New York City. Many cities have already adopted shorter hours for firefighters, others will follow soon.

1920
* Prohibition in effect with 18th Amendment.
* September 16 - Wall Street explosion; 40 killed.

1921
* California passes a law forbidding wooden shingles on roofs but pressure from the roofing industry brings a repeal.
* Tulsa, OK race riot produces fire over 35 city blocks, destroying over 1250 residences.

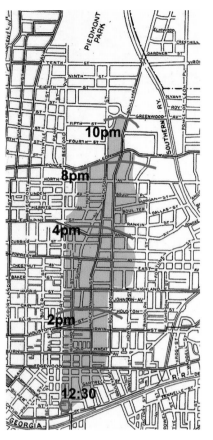

Map of fire damage in Atlanta, GA.

Race riot fires in Tulsa, OK.

1922
* President Warren Harding issues first Fire Prevention Week proclamation.
* Standards for Municipal Fire Alarm systems are adopted.
* December 8 - Fire destroys 30 blocks in the center of Astoria, OR during a rainstorm.
* December 20 - Last horse-drawn engine in New York City is retired.

1923
* Cleveland School Fire in Beulah, SC results in 77 deaths.
* Tokyo and Yokohama earthquake and conflagration in Japan - approximately 91,344 lose their lives.
* United States Chamber of Commerce sponsors National Fire Waste Council with contest for fire prevention in cities by local chambers of commerce.
* Fire prevention education in schools required by thirteen states.
* September 17 - Brush fire roars through Berkeley, CA and destroys 640 buildings.

1926
* Shakespeare Memorial Theater burns in Stratford-on-Avon, England (birthplace to William Shakespeare).

1927
* "The Jazz Singer," the first sound movie, thrills audiences.
* Lindbergh flies from New York to Paris.
* Annual Fire Prevention Week inaugurated.

1928
* Fire in Fall River, MA burns 107 factories and countless business blocks.

Berkeley, CA brush fires in 1923

1929
* May 15 - Cleveland Clinic Fire. Approximately 125 are killed when X-ray films burn and give off poisonous fumes. As a result of this fire, new laws require the use of "safety film."
* The Stock Market Crash. The great depression has devastating effects on fire department budgets, resulting in losses of manpower and stations. Arson fires increase.

1930
* Ohio State Penitentiary fire, Columbus, OH claims the lives of 320.

1930-1933
* Comprehensive fire loss study estimates that most fire deaths involving the very old and the very young occur in ordinary dwellings.

1934
* Conflagration in Hakodate, Japan destroys one-half of the city and takes 2018 lives.

Cleveland Clinic fire in 1929

* Woolworth building fire in Aurora, IL. Three firefighters are killed and six others are injured when a wall collapses.
* S.S. Morro Castle catches fire off the New Jersey coast, 134 killed.
* May 19 - Chicago Stockyards Fire.
* Fire destroys 20 blocks in the center of Nome, AK on September 17th.

1936
* Crystal Palace in England burns to the ground. Originally built in 1851 for the Great Exhibition held in London's Hyde Park.

1937
* Consolidated School fire in New London, TX is a gas explosion claiming 294 lives. This fire focused attention on the need to safeguard buildings not subject to municipal ordinances.
* The world famous German zeppelin "Hindenburg" burns as a result of an engine spark igniting flammable hydrogen, resulting in 36 deaths in Linderhurst, NJ.

New London, TX school explosion in 1937

1939
* World War II begins. Incendiary bombs dropped on European cities.

1941
* December 7 – The surprise bombing of Pearl Harbor by the Japanese results in the loss of 2383 lives and 19 American ships. Other losses - $25 million damage to aircraft, $25 million damage to buildings, supplies and ammunitions, 88 ships damaged and 960 persons missing. The Pearl Harbor experience leads to the fire training program of the U.S. Navy.
* Japanese and European cities continue to be destroyed by war conflagrations.

1942
* November 28 - Coconut Grove Night Club fire, Boston, MA resulting in 492 deaths. This fire shows the need for practical improvements. Underwriter Laboratories steps up research on combustibles in public places.

Coconut Grove Night Club fire in Boston, MA.

1943
* "Rain of Terror" in Hamburg, Germany. British fire storm bombings kill 60,000 to 100,000 people.

1944
* "Smokey Bear" character created to publicize the need to prevent forest fires.
* Gas explosion and fire at the East Ohio Gas Co. in Cleveland, OH causes 130 deaths.
* Munitions Depot explosion in Port Chicago, CA results in 300 deaths.
* July 6 - The Ringling Bros. and Barnum &

Bailey circus tent catches fire in Hartford, CT with 167 people being killed and nearly 500 injured.

Circus fire in Hartford, CT in 1944

1945
* Dresden, Germany, suffers explosive incendiary bomb raid, resulting in 300,000 deaths.
* Extensive fire bombing of Tokyo by Allied aircraft.
* Eastern Air Lines DC-3 near Florence, S.C., fire in flight results in 22 deaths.
* Empire State Building struck by Army Air Corps B-25, leaving 14 dead.
* May 7 - Germany surrenders.
* August 14 - Japan surrenders after atom bombs are dropped on Hiroshima and Nagasaki, Japan, signaling the end of World War II.

1946
* June 5 - Sixty-one die in a fire at the LaSalle Hotel fire, Chicago, IL.
* December 7 - Winecoff Hotel fire in Atlanta, GA results in 119 deaths.

1947
* The Markay, a petroleum tanker, catches fire in Los Angeles, CA. Fireboats used to fight miles of waterfront fire.

Tanker Markay on LA waterfront

* October 23 – Raging forest fires burn in Maine, destroying 1200 buildings and killing 16.

* April 16 - Ammonium nitrate being loaded on the S.S. Grandcamp explodes in Texas City, TX. More than 600 are killed, including the entire membership of the volunteer fire department.
* Centralia Coal Co., Centralia, IL dust explosion claims 111 deaths.

1948
* DC-4 airplane accident at Chicago Municipal Airport (now Midway) results in 12 deaths. This

Texas City fire destroys fire department

fire recognizes the need for specialized aircraft rescue and fire fighting vehicles for airports.
* The US Postal Service issues a three-cent stamp honoring volunteer firefighters.

1951
* "Sparky the Fire Dog" created as a symbol of fire prevention for children.

1954
* Cleveland Hill School fire, Cheektowaga, NY leaves 15 dead.
* Oil refinery fire in Whiting, IN results in $16 million loss, explosion and boil over.
* Junior Fire Department in Los Angeles, CA organized.
* Larkin Building fire is the first fire in Buffalo, NY history to go to a general alarm.

1958
* Our Lady of Angels School, Chicago, IL, rubbish fire spreads through open stairway resulting in 95 deaths. Major revisions in school construction and maintenance codes result.

Our Lady of Angels school fire in 1958

1965
* Multiple fires resulting from Watts racial riots in Los Angeles, CA. After 34 lives were lost, special gear was used to protect firefighters as a defense.

Apollo 1 damage

1967
* January 16 - Chicago McCormick Place fire, bringing 500 persons and 94 pieces of fire equipment to the scene.
* January 27 - Apollo 1 burns from an electrical fire during ground tests at Cape Kennedy, Florida; three astronauts - Virgil "Gus" Grissom, Edward White, and Roger Chafee - die in the blaze.
* A fire resistant fabric, Nomex®, is invented.
* U.S.S. Forrestal aircraft carrier fire off coast of Vietnam results in 131 deaths.

1975
* A B-727 plane crashes and burns in New York. Spilled fuel ignites after the crash, causing 113 deaths.

1976
* Social Club fire in Bronx, New York claims 25 lives.
* Nursing home fire in Chicago, IL results in 24 deaths.

1977
* Fire at the "Beverly Hills Supper Club" in Southgate, KY results in 165 deaths.

1980
* MGM Hotel fire in Las Vegas, NV claims the lives of 85 people.

Beverly Hills Supper Club fire in KY

* Stouffer's Inn Hotel fire, Harrison, NY claims 26 victims.
* May 18 - Mount St. Helens, WA erupts, making it the most deadly and economically destructive volcanic event in the history of the United States. The eruption claimed fifty-seven lives, and destroyed 250 homes, 47 bridges, 15 miles of railways and 185 miles of highways.

1983
* North Division street explosion in Buffalo, NY takes the lives of five firefighters and two civilians while destroying millions of dollars in property.

Charred slot machines at the MGM Grand

1986
* January 28 - the Space Shuttle Challenger lifts off at 11:38 a.m. EST. Seventy three seconds into the mission, the Challenger explodes, killing the entire crew of seven astronauts.

1990
*August 9 - Yosemite National Park closed due to three widespread wildland fires.
* Severe drought causes August fires in parts of Alaska, Idaho, Oregon, Utah and Washington State. Nearly 20,000 firefighters work at containing fires that cover 856,000 acres, more than half of that acreage being in Alaska.

Satellite photo of Yosemite Park fire

Oil fires in Kuwait

1991

*April 19 - Waco, TX, where intentional fires are set in the Branch Davidian religious sect compound, killing an estimated 76 cultists including 21 children.

* Saddam Hussein sets Kuwait oil wells on fire. Fire fighting teams from all over the world, including famed firefighter Red Adair, fight these fires for months trying to save the oil resources, as well as reduce air pollution.

1993

* Windsor Castle, just west of London, England, the largest inhabited castle in the world and one of the official residences of the British monarch, Queen Elizabeth II, suffers severe damage in a fire, destroying some of the most historic parts of the building.

1995

* Oklahoma City Bombing by American terrorists leaves 169 dead.

2000

* Week long raging windswept fires cause evacuation of 11,000 residents of Los Alamos, NM, and declaration as a disaster area by President Clinton.

2001

* September 11 - Foreign terrorists attack the World Trade Center in New York City and the Pentagon in Washington DC. The Pentagon attack results in 189 deaths. In New York, both of the 110-story towers collapse, killing nearly 3000, including 344 firefighters and 87 police officers. A fourth hijacked plane, United Flight 93, crashs in rural Pennsylvania, leaving no survivors out of the 40 crew members and passengers.

Satellite photo of aftermath from 9/11

Lots & Lots of FIRE TRUCKS & FIREFIGHTERS

2005

* August finds hundreds of firefighters battling several heat-fueled forest fires that rage across Spain and Portugal amid a severe drought that dried reservoirs and lead to water restrictions in many places. Over 1700 firefighters and soldiers, backed by 22 water-dropping aircraft and 359 vehicles, are involved in the firefighting operation in Portugal, which along with Spain, faces its worst dry spell since the 1940's.

2006

* As of the end of September, there have been about 84,000 wildland fires across the lower 48 States since the beginning of 2006, and over 9 million acres have burned, according to estimates from the National Interagency Fire Center. The preliminary number of acres burned so far in the U.S. is a record for an entire year. Over half of the fires and a quarter of the burned acreage occur in the Southern Area, which encompasses 13 states, Puerto Rico, the Virgin Islands and the District of Columbia.

Forest fires in Spain

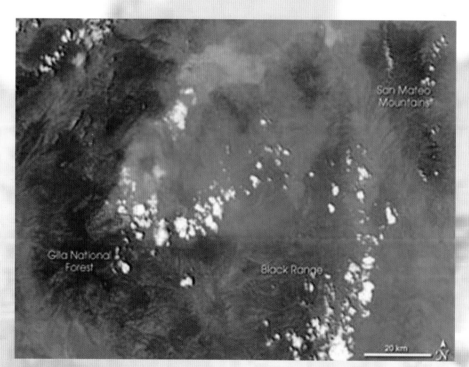

Wildfires in Western New Mexico, 2006

Fire Museums with sites on the World Wide Web

We have attempted to list links of all Fire Museums with Websites, as well as a few related Websites of general historical interest. For a more complete list of the over 300 Fire Truck Museums in the world please visit the website of the Fire Museum Network at http://www.firemuseumnetwork.org/index.html

About the Fire Museum Network

The Fire Museum Network is a nonprofit entity which provides a means for networking among fire museums and promotes the interests of those dedicated to collecting, preserving, and interpreting the artifacts, history, and traditions of the fire service. An all-volunteer board of directors, elected from among the network membership, is responsible for planning the annual Fire Museum Seminar, updating the website and administering to the affairs of the organization.

Directory of Fire Museums

Ranging from the spare room in a firehouse basement to magnificent first-class institutions with warehouse-like proportions, there are close to 300 museums which preserve and celebrate the glorious heritage of firefighting in North America. Collectively, these institutions serve to inform, educate, and inspire us all. Plan an individual trip or a group outing - it's a lot of fun!

(Note: From time to time, new museums may open, while others may close their doors or discontinue their websites. This listing is the most accurate available at the time of printing.)

Alabama

- Phoenix Fire Museum - Mobile, Alabama

http://www.ci.mobile.al.us/dept/museum/museum.htm

Alaska

- Valdez Museum & Historical Archive - Valdez, Alaska

http://www.alaska.net/~vldzmuse/index.html

Arizona

- Hall of Flame - Phoenix, Arizona

http://www.hallofflame.org

California

- African-American Firefighter Museum - Los Angeles California

http://www.lafd.org/aafm.htm

- Benicia Fire Museum - Benicia California

http://www.beniciafiremuseum.org/

- County of Los Angeles Fire Museum Association - Los Angeles Co. California

http://www.clafma.org

- California Fire Museum - Corona Del Mar, California

www.californiafiremuseum.org

- Fire Memories (a museum) - Indio, California

http://www.firememories.org

- Firehouse Museum - San Diego, California

http://www.globalinfo.com/noncomm/firehouse/Firehouse.html

- Glendale Fire Department Museum - Glendale, California

http://fire.ci.glendale.ca.us/museum/museum.html

- The Haggin Museum - Stockton, California

http://www.hagginmuseum.org/

- Monterey Fire Department Historical Museum - Monterey, California

http://www.monterey.org/fire/museum.html

- Pioneer Mutual Hook & Ladder Society Sacramento, California

http://www.rcip.com/pmhls

- San Francisco Fire Museum - San Francisco, California

http://www.sffiremuseum.org

- San Francisco Firehouse Tour (includes historic firehouses and the fire museum)- San Francisco, California

http://www.firehousetours.com

- San Jose Fire Museum - San Jose, California

http://www.sanjosefiremuseum.com

Colorado

- Denver Firefighters Museum - Denver, Colorado

http://www.denverfirefightersmuseum.org

- Friends of Dr. Lester L. Williams Fire Museum - Colorado Springs, Colorado

http://www.fire-museum.com

- Red, White, & Blue Fire Co. Museum - Breckenridge, Colorado

http://www.rwbfire.org/Museum/museum.htm

- Reliance Fire Company Museum - Estes Park, Colorado

http://www.reliancefiremuseum.org

Connecticut

- Bethel Historical Firefighters Museum - Bethel, Connecticut

http://users.erols.com/gorval/mus.htm

- Connecticut Fire Museum - East Windsor, Connecticut

http://www.ctfiremuseum.org/

- The Fire Museum - Manchester, Connecticut

http://www.thefiremuseum.org

Manchester Fire Museum

Delaware

- Christiana Fire Company Museum - Christiana, Delaware

http://www.magpage.com/~smokey/history.html

Florida

- Fort Lauderdale Fire and Safety Museum - Fort Lauderdale, Florida

http://fortlauderdalefiremuseum.com

- Orlando Fire Department Museum (Old Fire Sta. 3) - Orlando, Florida

http://www.geocities.com/dickcamnitz/museum1.html

- Tampa Fire Museum - Tampa, Florida

http://www.tampagov.net/dept_Fire_Museum/

Illinois

- Aurora Regional Fire Museum - Aurora, Illinois

http://www.auroraregionalfiremuseum.org

Aurora Regional Fire Museum

- Chicago History Museum - Chicago, Illinois

http://www.chicagohs.org/

- Fire Museum of Greater Chicago - Chicago, Illinois

http://www.firemuseumofgreaterchicago.org/

- Illinois State Fire Museum - Springfield, Illinois

http://www.state.il.us/osfm/museum.htm

- Northern Illinois Fire Museum - Marengo, Illinois

http://www.nifm.net

Idaho

- Idaho Forset Fire Museum - Moscow, Idaho

http://www.woodlandgifts.com/museum.php?

Indiana

- Fort Wayne Firefighters Museum Inc. - Fort Wayne, Indiana

http://www.ftwaynefiremuseum.com

- Indianapolis Fire Dept. - Links to Fire Museum and Survive Alive House - Indianapolis, Indiana

http://www.ci.indianapolis.in.us/ifd/

Iowa

- Clear Lake Fire Museum - Clear Lake, Iowa

http://www.clearlakeiowa.com/html/thin.html

- International Fire Museum - Davenport, Iowa

http://www.artcom.com/museums/nv/gl/52803-37.htm

Kansas

- Kansas Fire Museum - Wichita, Kansas

http://members.cox.net/ksfm/

- Traditions Fire Company and Museum - Olathe, Kansas

http://traditionsfireco.org

Kentucky

- Appalachian Foothills Fire Historical Society - Barbourville, Kentucky

http://www.geocities.com/affhs

Louisiana

- Baton Rouge Fire Museum - Baton Rouge, Louisiana

http://www.intersurf.com/%7Eaevinc/aev2see.htm

- New Orleans Fire Museum - New Orleans, Louisiana

http://www.cityofno.com/portal.aspx?portal=51&tabid=10

- Shreveport Fire Fighter's Museum - Shreveport, Louisiana

http://www.softdisk.com/comp/classic/

Maine

- Hose 5 Fire Museum. - Bangor Maine

http://www.bgrme.org/ index.php3?c1=government_operations&c2=fire&c3=hose5_museum

- Freeport Fire and Rescue Department Museum - Freeport, Maine

http:// www.datoys.com/ freeport-fr- museum.htm

Hose 5 Fire Museum

Maryland

- Fire Museum of Maryland - Baltimore, Maryland

http://www.firemuseummd.org

- Gaithersburg - Washington Grove VFD Fire Museum - Gaithersburg, Maryland

http://www.gwgvfd.org/museum.cfm

Massachusetts

- <u>Bare Cove Fire Museum - Hingham, Massachusetts</u>

http://www.barecovefiremuseum.org/

- <u>Brockton Fire Museum - Brockton, Massachusetts</u>

http://www.brocktonma.com/bhs/firemus.html

- <u>Boston Fire Museum - Boston, Massachusetts</u>

http://www.bostonfiremuseum.com

Boston Fire Museum

- <u>Haverhill Fire Dept. Fire Fighting Museum - Haverhill, Massachusetts</u>

http://www.hfdffm.org

- <u>New Bedford Fire Museum - New Bedford, Massachusetts</u>

http://www.ci.new-bedford.ma.us/PSAFETY/FIRE/MUSEUM.htm

- <u>Peabody Historical Fire Museum - Peabody, Massachusetts</u>

http://www.peabodyhistorical.org/museum.htm

- <u>Lexington Antique Fire Equipment Museum - Lexington, Massachusetts</u>

http://www.lexingtonhistory.org/museum2.html

- <u>Old Firehouse Museum - South Hadley, Massachusetts</u>

http://www.southhadley.org/firehouse.htm

Michigan

- <u>Michigan Firehouse Museum - Ypsilanti, Michigan</u>

http://www.michiganfirehousemuseum.org

- <u>Wolverine Fire Co. - Battle Creek, Michigan</u>

http://my.voyager.net/wolvfireco/index.html

Minnesota

- <u>Bill & Bonnie Daniels Firefighters Hall & Museum - Minneapolis, Minnesota</u>

http://www.firehallmuseum.org

Mississippi

- <u>American Heritage "Big Red" Fire Museum - Louisville, Mississippi</u>

http://www.taylorbigred.com/fire_museum.html

- <u>Jackson Public Fire education Ctr. & Fire Museum - Jackson, Mississippi</u>

http://city.jackson.ms.us/Fire/pfsed_museum.html

- <u>Old Firehouse Museum - Greenville, Mississippi</u>

http://www.greenville.ms.us/museums/fires.html

Greenville Old Firehouse Museum

Missouri

- Fire Museum of Missouri - Willow Springs Missouri

http://www.usfirehouse.com/

- First Due Fire Museum - Hazelwood Missouri

http://www.firstduefiremuseum.com

Nevada

- Firefighters Museum of Nevada - Las Vegas, Nevada

http://www.wizard.com/~pauly/ffmn.html

- Liberty Engine Company No. 1, The Comstock Firemen's Museum - Virginia City, Nevada

http://www.comstockfiremuseum.com/

Comstock Firemen's Museum

- Reno Fire Department Museum - Reno, Nevada

http://www.ci.reno.nv.us/pub_safety/fire/admin/museum/

- Warren Engine Company No. 1 Museum - Carson City, Nevada

http://www.carson-city.nv.us/CCFD/weco/2.htm

New Hampshire

- Always Ready Engine House - Hollis, New Hampshire

http://www.hollis-history.org/enginehouse.htm

- Derry Firefighters' Museum - Derry New Hampshire

http://www.derryfire.org/Stations/
Derry_Firefighters_Museum.htm

- Seacoast Fire Museum - Hampton New Hampshire

http://www.hamptonhistoricalsociety.org/fire.htm

New Jersey

- Bayonne Firefighters Museum - Bayonne, New Jersey

http://www.bayonnenj.org/museum.htm

- Friendship Fire Company Museum - Woodbury, New Jersey

http://www.jersey.net/~dwayne/history1.htm

- Fireworks-USA - New Jersey State Fire Engine Museum

http://www.fireworks-usa.org

New Mexico

- Wildland Firefighter Museum - Capitan New Mexico

http://www.wildlandfirefighter.net/

New York

- Brookhaven Town Volunteer Firefighters Museum - Ridge New York

http://www.brookhavenfiremuseum.org

Brookhaven Fire Museum

- Buffalo Fire Historical Society - Buffalo, New York

http://www.geocities.com/buffalofirehistoricalsociety

- FASNY Museum of Fire Fighting - Hudson, New York

http:// www.fasnyfiremuseum.com

- The Historic 1897 Firehouse - Elmira, New York

http://www.elmirafiremuseum.org

- Homeville Antique Fire Dept. - Homer, New York

http://members.aol.com/mijfire/home.htm

- Nassau County Firefighters Museum & Ed. Ctr. - Garden City, New York

http://www.ncfiremuseum.org/

- New York City Fire Museum - New York, New York

http://nycfiremuseum.org

- Rockland County Volunteer Fire Services Museum - Pomona, New York

http://rcfiremuseum.org

- Orange County Museum - Montgomery, New York

http://www.ocfm.us

- Vol. Firemen's Hall & Museum of Kingston - Kingston, New York

http://www.ci.kingston.ny.us/Tourism/Museums.html#Fire

- Yonkers Fire Museum - Yonkers, New York

http://www.yonkersfiremuseum.org

North Carolina

- American LaFrance Museum - Cleveland, North Carolina

http://www.americanlafrance.com/Museum/

- Charlotte-Mecklenburg Fire Ed. Ctr. & Museum - Charlotte, North Carolina

http://www.charlottefiremuseum.com/

- Kings Mountain Fire Dept. Hist. Fire Museum - Kings Mountain, North Carolina

http://www.kmfire.com/fire_museum.htm

- New Bern Fiemen's Museum - New Bern, North Carolina

http://www4.coastalnet.com/newbern/psafepg6.htm

Ohio

- Central Insurance Companies Fire Museum - Van Wert, Ohio

http://www.central-insurance.com/docs/museum.htm

- Central Ohio Fire Museum & Learning Center - Columbus, Ohio

http://www.fire.ci.columbus.oh.us/museum.htm

- Cincinnati Fire Museum - Cincinnati, Ohio

www.cincyfiremuseum.com

- Firefighters Memorial Museum - Lima, Ohio

http://www.limafiremuseum.org

Firefighters Memorial Museum, Lima

- Mentor Fire Museum - Mentor Ohio

http://www.angelfire.com/oh5/mentorfiremuseum

- Toledo Firefighters Museum - Toledo, Ohio

http://www.toledofiremuseum.com

- Western Reserve Fire Museum and Ed. Center - Cleveland Ohio

http://www.wrfmc.com

Oklahoma

- Oklahoma Firefighters Museum - Oklahoma City, Oklahoma

http://www.brightok.net/~osfa/

Oregon

- Albany Fire Museum - Albany, Oregon

http://www.ohwy.com/or/a/albanyfm.htm

- Oregon Fire Service Museum and Learning Center - Salem, Oregon

http://www.oregonfiremuseum.com

- Uppertown Firefighters Museum - Astoria, Oregon

http://www.ohwy.com/or/u/upfiremu.htm

Pennsylvania

- Firefighters' Historical Museum - Erie, Pennsylvania

http://www.firefightershistory.org

- Fireman's Hall - Philadelphia, Pennsylvania

http://www.ushistory.org/tour/tour_fireman.htm

- Fire Museum of Greater Harrisburg - Harrisburg, Pennsylvania

http://members.aol.com/JCW37/FRmuseum.html

Fire Museum of York County

- Fire Museum of York County - York, Pennsylvania

http://www.yorkheritage.org/fire_museum.html

- Hanover Fire Museum - Hanover, Pennsylvania

http://www.borough.hanover.pa.us/images/hanover/hbfiremuseum.html

- Greensburg Fire Museum - Greensburg, Pennsylvania

http://www.greensburgfire.org

- The Honesdale Fire Museum - Honesdale, Pennsylvania

http://www.engine3.org/Museum.html

- Manheim Fire Co. Museum - Manheim, Pennsylvania

http://www.manheimfire.com/museum.htm

- Philadelphia Contributionship Ins. Co. - Philadelphia, Pennsylvania

http://www.contributionship.com/

- Reading Area Fire Museum - Reading, Pennsylvania

http://www.readingpafire.com/museum/museum.htm

- Schuylkill Historical Fire Society - Shenandoah, Pennsylvania

http://www.462fd.com/SHFS/

- Union Fire Co. Museum - Carlisle, Pennsylvania

http://www.unionfireco.org/Museum_frame.htm

- Upland Fire Co. Museum - Upland, Pennsylvania

http://upland57.org

Rhode Island

- Jamestown Fire Museum - Jamestown, Rhode Island

http://members.aol.com/kacie333/mus.htm

South Carolina

- Columbia Fire Museum - Columbia, South Carolina

http://www.columbiasouthcarolina.com/fire-museum.html

- South Carolina Firefighters Museum

http://www.scfm2000.org

Tennessee

- Fire Museum of Memphis - Memphis, Tennessee

http://www.firemuseum.com

Texas

- Houston Fire Museum - Houston, Texas

http://www.houstonfiremuseum.org/

Texas Fire Museum

- Fire Museum of Texas - Beaumont, Texas

http://www.cityofbeaumont.com/Fire.htm#f muse

- Texas Fire Museum - Dallas, Texas

http://www.texasfiremuseum.org

Utah Museum of Fire Service History
& Firefighter Memorial

Utah

- Utah Museum of Fire Service History & Firefighter Memorial - Grantsville Utah

http://www.utahfiremuseum.com

Virginia

- Friendship Firehouse Museum - Alexandria, Virginia

http://ci.alexandria.va.us/oha/friendship/index.html

- Fire Fighters Museum of Central Virginia - Lynchburg, Virginia

http://www.firefightersmuseum.com

- Manassas Vol. Fire Co. - Fire Museum - Manassas, Virginia

http://www.manassasfire.com/museum.html

- The Virginia Fire and Police Museum - Richmond, Virginia

http://www.vafire-police.org

Washington

- Everett Firefighter's Hall & Fire Museum - Everett, Washington

http://www.everettfirefighters.org

- Washington Fire Lookout Museum - Spokane, Washington

http://www.firelookouts.com

- Yakima Valley Museum - Yakima, Washington

http://yakimavalleymuseum.org/community/index.html

Wisconsin

- Firehouse No. 3 Museum - Racine, Wisconsin

http://www.execpc.com/~vf/vf_fh3.htm

Old Firehouse and Police Museum

- Old Firehouse and Police Museum - Superior, Wisconsin

http://www.visitsuperior.com/history&museums.htm

- Milwaukee Fire Ed. Center & Museum, Milwaukee, Wisconsin

http://www.milfire.com/fire_museum.htm

Chapter 18
Cool Fire Related Websites

NATIONAL AGENCIES AND ORGANIZATIONS

National Fire Protection Agency
http://www.nfpa.org/

USDA Forest Service
www.fs.fed.us

U.S. Fire Administration (USFA)
http://www.usfa.dhs.gov

U.S. Fire Administration for Kids
www.usfa.dhs.gov/kids/flash.shtm

The International Association of Fire Chiefs
www.iafc.org

The International Association of Fire Fighters
www.iaff.org

U.S. Department of Homeland Security
www.dhs.gov/index.shtm

National Interagency Fire Center (NIFC)
http://www.nifc.gov/index.html

U.S. Fish & Wildlife Service
www.fws.gov/fire/

Bureau of Land Management/Office of
Fire and Aviation
http://www.fire.blm.gov/index.htm

National Park Service/U.S. Department of
the Interior
http://www.nps.gov/nifc/

USDA Forest Service
http://www.fs.fed.us/fire/

Wildland Firefighter Foundation
http://www.wffoundation.org

OSHA Fire Safety
www.allaboutosha.com/fire-safety-protection-prevention.html

National Fallen Firefighters Foundation
http://www.firehero.org

FIRE SITES FOR KIDS OF ALL AGES!

"Lots And Lots Of Fire Trucks"
www.lotsandlotsoffiretrucks.com

Federal Emergency Management Agency
www.fema.gov/kids/

Smokey Bear.com
www.smokeybear.com

Sparky the Fire Dog ®
www.sparky.org

Play Safe! Be Safe! Presented by BIC Corporation
www.playsafebesafe.com/

Sesame Street: Parent's Guide to Learning (Fire Safety)
www.sesameworkshop.org/parents/solutions/information/
listing.php?categoryId=30786&sectionKey=safety

Pierce Fire Truck Manufacturing –
Appleton, Wisconsin
www.piercemfg.com

Aurora Regional Fire Museum
www.auroraregionalfiremuseum.org

James Coffey Children's Music
www.bluevisionmusic.com

Exciting Fire Pictures!
www.torontofirepix.com

Mount St. Helens VolcanoCam
www.fs.fed.us/gpnf/volcanocams/msh/

Building Awareness Through Firefighter Life SafetyTraining
www.everyonegoeshome.com

Chapter 19

Lots of Fire Trucks Sing-A-Long Song Lyrics

Following are the words to the songs you'll find in our "LOTS AND LOTS OF FIRE TRUCKS" DVDs and music CD. We hope you'll watch the programs or listen to the CD and sing right along with Firefighter Joe, the kids, and award-winning song writer and composer James Coffey.

You can also find other wonderful music CD's and DVD's at www.bluevisionmusic.com and www.marshallpublishinginc.com

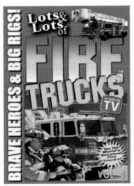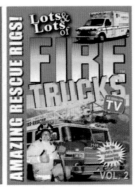

Lots & Lots of FIRE TRUCKS & FIREFIGHTERS

"Lots & Lots of Fire Trucks"
Words & Music by James Coffey © 2006 Blue Vision Music

(Verse 1)
Lots of Chrome and Shinin' Steel
Brave Men and Women Sit Behind
The Wheel
When They're On Their Way Everyone
Will Know
Hear The Motors Roar' And The
Sirens Blow

(Chorus)
I See Lots and Lots of Fire Trucks
I Can See Those Big Engines Roarin'
Down The Street
I See Lots and Lots of Fire Trucks
Here They Come Now Through The
Smoke And Heat
I Can See Those Big Engines Roarin' Down The Street

(Verse 2)
In A Fire Or Emergency
In Any Situation That Needs Urgency
They Are On The Job Both Day And Night
Fighting Fires 'Til The Morning Light

(Chorus)

(Verse 3)
They're Ready Anytime Or Anywhere
On The Ground, In The Water, Or In The Air
From The Southern States To Baltimore
From The Eastern Coast To The Western Shore

(Chorus)

"Great Big Fire Truck"
Words & Music by James Coffey © 2006 Blue Vision Music

Here they Come Roaring Down The Street
With Their Lights A Flashing Through The Blazing Heat
The Engines Roar And The Tires Squeal
The Need Is Urgent And The Danger's Real

Trouble Big Or Trouble Small
There's No Worries We Can Handle It All
If You Need Some Help Why You're In Luck
Because Here Comes A Great Big Fire Truck
When The Call Comes In They Are Out The Door
Never Really Knowing What Their Headed For
Racing The Streets And The Alleyways
Fighting A Path Through The Fiery Blaze

From The Biggest Fires To The Smallest Flame
Through The Wind And Heat And The Pouring Rain
If You Need Some Help Why You're In Luck
Because Here Comes A Great Big Fire Truck
From The Biggest Cities To The Smallest Towns
To The Tallest Building Or On The Ground
If You Have A Problem They'll Be Right There
Yes Anytime Or Anywhere

Clear The Way They're Coming Through
Brave Fire Fighters And Rescue Crews
If You Need Some Help Why You're In Luck
Because Here Comes A Great Big Fire
Truck
Here Comes A Great Big Fire Truck
Here Comes A Great Big Fire Truck

Lots & Lots of FIRE TRUCKS & FIREFIGHTERS

"Call 911"
Words & Music by James Coffey © 2006 Blue Vision Music

(Chorus)
Call 911 And Help Will Come
Don't Be Afraid It'll Be OK
You Call 911 And Help Will Come
Don't Be Afraid We Are On Our
Way

(Verse 1)
Ask Everyone In Your
Neighborhood
Are Your Smoke Detectors Working
Way They Should?
And In Case Of Emergency Understand
You Should Always Have A Safety Plan

(Chorus)
Call 911 And Help Will Come
Don't Be Afraid It'll Be OK
You Call 911 And Help Will Come
Don't Be Afraid Help We Are On Our Way

(Verse 2)
When The Fire Fighter Comes Here's What You Do
Listen Real Close So They Can Rescue You
Stay Real Calm And Keep Your Cool
Always Follow The Safety Rules

(Verse 3)
If You're On Fire Don't Lose Control
Just Remember To Stop, Drop And Roll!
Don't Play With Matches Of Any Kind
And If You See A Fire Don't Waste Time

(Chorus)
Call 911 And Help Will Come
Don't Be Afraid It'll Be OK
Just Call 911 And Help Will Come
Don't Be Afraid Help Is On The Way

Lots & Lots of FIRE TRUCKS & FIREFIGHTERS

"Heroes Brave And Tall"
Words & Music by James Coffey © 2006 Blue Vision Music

(Verse 1)
No Matter What The Cost
No Matter The Sacrifice
They Do What It Takes
No Matter What The Price
Who Will Lift You Up
When The Water Is Deep?
Who Will Lend You Strength
When Your Body's Weak?

(Chorus)
When Danger Calls
All You Need Is A Hero
Standing Brave And Tall
All Over The Land
When Darkness Falls
All You Need Is A Hero
An Angel Of Mercy...A Helping Hand

(Verse 2)
When You're Feeling Lost
They Will Help You Find Your Way
When The Others Run
They Won't Turn Away
Not The Raging Heat
Nor The Freezing Cold
Will Shake Their Nerves Of Steel
Nor Shatter Their Hearts Of Gold

(Chorus)

(Verse 3)
In The Darkest Times
They Will Shine A Light
When Everything Seems Wrong
They Will Do What's Right
Not Afraid To Fail

Not Too Afraid To Try
Holding On To Hope
Holding On To Life

(Chorus)

Lots & Lots of FIRE TRUCKS & FIREFIGHTERS

"It's An Emergency"
Words & Music by James Coffey © 2006 Blue Vision Music

Tires squeal
Chrome and steel
You can feel the heat
Coming down the street
It'll be alright
We're ready day or night
You can count on me

In an emergency
It's an emergency
It's an emergency
It's an emergency
It's an emergency

Fire or crime
Rain or shine
Large or small
We can handle it all
We are on the scene
With our rescue team
No need to fear because
Help is here

It's an emergency
It's an emergency
It's an emergency
It's an emergency

Days and night
Sirens and lights
Clear the avenue
We are coming through

In your home or car
No matter where you are
It'll be OK
We are on our way

It's an emergency
It's an emergency
It's an emergency
It's an emergency

Lots & Lots of FIRE TRUCKS & FIREFIGHTERS

Chapter 20

Conclusion

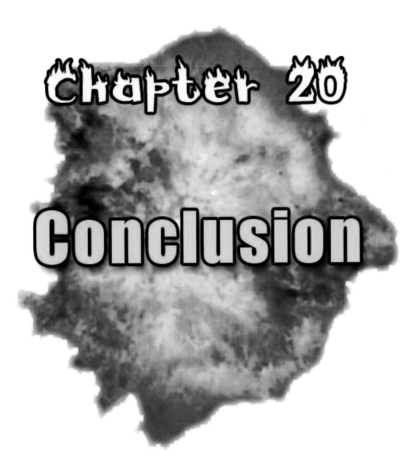

I hope this book has given you an idea of what my world is like.

Being a firefighter is a dangerous job, but it's also an extremely satisfying one. It gives me the chance to make a difference in people's lives. It's a job that keeps me fit – both physically and mentally. It's a job that keeps me in touch with the latest technology and some of the neatest equipment you've ever seen.

I've never had any regrets about choosing this career – I'm proud of the heritage that firefighting carries, I'm proud of the camaraderie and closeness that being a firefighter brings to the firehouse, and I'm proud to put my life on the line, every time the fire alarm rings.

The next time you hear a fire engine roar by, or the wail of an ambulance siren, just remember folks like me – Firefighter Joe.

Thanks.

Lots & Lots of FIRE TRUCKS & FIREFIGHTERS

Lots & Lots of FIRE TRUCKS & FIREFIGHTERS